Max Lucado

Life Lessons *from*

1 & 2 Peter

Between the Rock and a Hard Place

Prepared by The Livingstone Corporation

Thomas Nelson
Since 1798

CONTENTS

HOW TO STUDY THE BIBLE

The Bible is a peculiar book. Words crafted in another language. Deeds done in a distant era. Events recorded in a far-off land. Counsel offered to a foreign people. It is a peculiar book.

It's surprising that anyone reads it. It's too old. Some of its writings date back 5,000 years. It's too bizarre. The book speaks of incredible floods, fires, earthquakes, and people with supernatural abilities. It's too radical. The Bible calls for undying devotion to a carpenter who called himself God's Son.

Logic says this book shouldn't survive. Too old, too bizarre, too radical.

The Bible has been banned, burned, scoffed, and ridiculed. Scholars have mocked it as foolish. Kings have branded it as illegal. A thousand times over the grave has been dug and the dirge has begun, but somehow the Bible never stays in the grave. Not only has it survived, but it has also thrived. It is the single most popular book in all of history. It has been the bestselling book in the world for years!

There is no way on earth to explain it. Which perhaps is the only explanation. For the Bible's durability is not found on *earth* but in *heaven*. The millions who have tested its claims and claimed its promises know there is but one answer: the Bible is God's book and God's voice.

As you read it, you would be wise to give some thought to two questions: *What is the purpose of the Bible?* and *How do I study the Bible?* Time spent reflecting on these two issues will greatly enhance your Bible study.

What is the purpose of the Bible?

Let the Bible itself answer that question: *"From infancy you have known the Holy Scriptures, which are able to make you wise for salvation through faith in Christ Jesus"* (2 Timothy 3:15).

The purpose of the Bible? Salvation. God's highest passion is to get his children home. His book, the Bible, describes his plan of salvation. The purpose of the Bible is to proclaim God's plan and passion to save his children.

This is the reason why this book has endured through the centuries. It dares to tackle the toughest questions about life: *Where do I go after I die? Is there a God? What do I do with my fears?* The Bible is the treasure map that leads to God's highest treasure—eternal life.

But how do you study the Bible? Countless copies of Scripture sit unread on bookshelves and nightstands simply because people don't know how to read it. What can you do to make the Bible real in your life?

The clearest answer is found in the words of Jesus: *"Ask and it will be given to you; seek and you will find; knock and the door will be opened to you"* (Matthew 7:7).

The first step in understanding the Bible is asking God to help you. You should read it prayerfully. If anyone understands God's Word, it is because of God and not the reader.

"The Advocate, the Holy Spirit, whom the Father will send in my name, will teach you all things and will remind you of everything I have said to you" (John 14:26).

Before reading the Bible, pray and invite God to speak to you. Don't go to Scripture looking for your idea, but go searching for his.

Not only should you read the Bible prayerfully, but you should also read it carefully. *"Seek and you will find"* is the pledge. The Bible is not a newspaper to be skimmed but rather a mine to be quarried. *"If you look for it as for silver and search for it as for hidden treasure, then you will understand the fear of the Lord and find the knowledge of God"* (Proverbs 2:4–5).

Any worthy find requires effort. The Bible is no exception. To understand the Bible, you don't have to be brilliant, but you must be willing to roll up your sleeves and search.

"Do your best to present yourself to God as one approved, a worker who does not need to be ashamed and who correctly handles the word of truth" (2 Timothy 2:15).

Here's a practical point. Study the Bible a bit at a time. Hunger is not satisfied by eating twenty-one meals in one sitting once a week. The body needs a steady diet to remain strong. So does the soul. When God sent food to his people in the wilderness, he didn't provide loaves already made. Instead, he sent them manna in the shape of *"thin flakes like frost on the ground"* (Exodus 16:14).

God gave manna in limited portions.

God sends spiritual food the same way. He opens the heavens with just enough nutrients for today's hunger. He provides *"a rule for this, a rule for that; a little here, a little there"* (Isaiah 28:10).

Don't be discouraged if your reading reaps a small harvest. Some days a lesser portion is all that is needed. What is important is to search every day for that day's message. A steady diet of God's Word over a lifetime builds a healthy soul and mind.

It's much like the little girl who returned from her first day at school feeling a bit dejected. Her mom asked, "Did you learn anything?"

"Apparently not enough," the girl responded. "I have to go back tomorrow, and the next day, and the next . . . "

Such is the case with learning. And such is the case with Bible study. Understanding comes little by little over a lifetime.

There is a third step in understanding the Bible. After the asking and seeking comes the knocking. After you ask and search, *"knock and the door will be opened to you"* (Matthew 7:7).

To knock is to stand at God's door. To make yourself available. To climb the steps, cross the porch, stand at the doorway, and volunteer. Knocking goes beyond the realm of thinking and into the realm of acting.

To knock is to ask, *What can I do? How can I obey? Where can I go?*

It's one thing to know what to do. It's another to do it. But for those who do it—those who choose to obey—a special reward awaits them.

"Whoever looks intently into the perfect law that gives freedom, and continues in it—not forgetting what they have heard, but doing it—they will be blessed in what they do" (James 1:25).

What a promise. Blessings come to those who do what they read in God's Word! It's the same with medicine. If you only read the label but ignore the pills, it won't help. It's the same with food. If you only read the recipe but never cook, you won't be fed. And it's the same with the Bible. If you only read the words but never obey, you'll never know the joy God has promised.

Ask. Search. Knock. Simple, isn't it? So why don't you give it a try? If you do, you'll see why the Bible is the most remarkable book in history.

The Books of 1 and 2 Peter

1 PETER

The science teacher makes a derisive statement about God creating the world. You raise your hand and state your convictions. Your teacher rolls her eyes. The students behind you chuckle.

It's not easy being the only one in your family who goes to church. It's bad enough that they don't go. It's worse that they make fun of you for going.

If you would pad your expense account, so could the other salesmen. But if you don't, they can't. "Come on," they urge you. "Just hedge a little." You refuse. The next day someone has spilled paint on your car.

Persecution. Not by firing squad. Not by death threats. Not by the government. But it's persecution nonetheless. A more subtle persecution. Persecution from friends, family, and peers. They won't take your life . . . but they will take your peace . . . and they'd like to take your faith, if you'll let them.

How do you respond? Begin with Peter's survival manual. He understood persecution. Beaten and jailed. Threatened and punished. He knew the sting of the false word and the angry whip. No doubt he'd seen some

Christians stand and others fall. He'd seen enough to know what it takes to stay strong in tough times.

His counsel may surprise you.

His counsel may sustain you. It may be just what you need so that "the genuineness of your faith, being much more precious than gold that perishes, though it is tested by fire, may be found to praise, honor, and glory at the revelation of Jesus Christ" (1 Peter 1:7 NKJV).

AUTHOR AND DATE

Peter, who along with James and John was a member of Jesus' "inner circle of disciples." As such, he was given access to the raising of Jairus' daughter (see Luke 8:49–51), Jesus' Transfiguration (see Matthew 17:1–2), and Jesus' agony in the Garden of Gethsemane (see Mark 14:32–34). Peter, along with his brother, Andrew, were fishermen when Jesus called them (see Matthew 4:18–20). His original name was Simon, but Jesus changed it to "Peter," which in Greek means "rock." Peter is perhaps best known for walking on the water (see Matthew 14:28–31), cutting off the ear of the high priest's servant at Jesus' arrest (see John 18:10), denying Christ (see Luke 22:54–62), and delivering a sermon on the Day of Pentecost that resulted in 3,000 people joining the church (see Acts 2:1–41). Peter likely composed the thoughts for his letter c. AD 64 from Rome, while Silas did the actual writing (see 1 Peter 5:12).

SITUATION

Peter addresses his letter to "the exiles scattered throughout" the northern region of Asia Minor (1:1), which most likely refers to a mixed group of Gentile and Jewish believers from a variety of different social backgrounds. These believers were enduring a form of persecution (though evidently not as a result of a state-induced policy) and were in need of encouragement from the disciple to follow the example of Christ and persevere in their faith. Peter's primary purposes in writing the letter are to remind his readers that they are (1) God's called and holy people (see 1:2), (2) strangers and sojourners in this world (see 2:9–10), and (3) people of faith whose sufferings for Christ will one day be vindicated and rewarded (see 4:12–14 and 5:4).

KEY THEMES

- Our richest inheritance is not in this world—it waits in heaven.
- It is up to each Christian to remain pure.
- It is an honor to suffer for Christ.
- Satan fights against the growth and victory of believers.

KEY VERSE

But in your hearts revere Christ as Lord. Always be prepared to give an answer to everyone who asks you to give the reason for the hope that you have (1 Peter 3:15).

CONTENTS

2 PETER

If a friend warns you, it's one thing. If a doctor warns you, you listen. But if your friend is your doctor, you lean forward and take note.

My friend is my doctor. My doctor is my friend. Most of my physical exams are salted with friendly chatter and jokes. There have been occasions, however, when his tone gets solemn and his voice urgent.

"We're going to have to watch this, Max."

"You haven't been exercising, have you . . ."

"With your family's history, you have to watch your diet."

When it's a warning from a friend, you listen.

The second letter from Peter is a warning from a friend. His first letter was a warning about trials from without (persecution). His second caution is a warning about trials from within (heresy).

In this, the last letter we have from him, he urges Christians to be careful. Avoid shortsightedness. Be on guard for false teachers. And, most importantly, be vigilant against personal complacency, which will lead to a lazy faith.

The doctor's task is to detect concerns from within and urge you to take caution. Peter's task is the same. Heed his counsel.

AUTHOR AND DATE

The author of this letter refers to himself as "Simon Peter, a servant and apostle of Christ," and historical evidence suggests the majority of early church fathers (including Cyril of Jerusalem, Jerome, and Augustine) accepted it as being from the disciple Peter. Furthermore, the author states that he was an eyewitness to the events of Jesus' life (see 1:14–18), that this is his "second letter" to his readers (3:1), and that the apostle Paul was his "dear brother" (3:15). Peter most likely wrote this second letter a few years after his first epistle, c. AD 67, and likely again from Rome, since the early church held that he was martyred in that city c. AD 68.

SITUATION

Peter provides fewer clues regarding the recipients of this letter, address it to a general audience of "those who through the righteousness of our God and Savior Jesus Christ have received a faith as precious as ours" (1:1). However, given that he notes this is his second letter, it can be assumed his recipients are the same group of believers from Asia Minor to which he wrote his first epistle. As with the first letter, it is likely the thoughts in this letter are from Peter, but that another person (fluent in Greek) actually wrote the letter. Also, given the fact the language and style of writing in 2 Peter varies greatly from 1 Peter, it is believed the disciple used a different writer (not Silas). Peter knows his time is drawing to a close, and his purpose in writing is to encourage the believers to persevere, remind them of the basis of their faith, compel them to instruct future generations in the faith, and warn against false teachers.

KEY THEMES

- The Scriptures were divinely inspired.
- There will be a great accountability in the final days when Jesus returns and God judges.
- It is utterly important to teach God's truth, purely and without addition.

KEY VERSE

The Lord is not slow in keeping his promise, as some understand slowness. Instead he is patient with you, not wanting anyone to perish, but everyone to come to repentance (2 Peter 3:9).

CONTENTS

A LIVING HOPE

Blessed be the God and Father of our Lord Jesus Christ, who according to His abundant mercy has begotten us again to a living hope through the resurrection of Jesus Christ from the dead.
1 PETER 1:3 NKJV

REFLECTION

It may just be a coincidence that *hope* and *cope* rhyme, but it's a happy coincidence. If we can't see beyond our immediate circumstances in life, the outlook quickly turns to a shade of despair. Consider a time, recently or in the past, when you felt hopeless about a situation in your life. How did you cope? What would have helped you during that time?

SITUATION

Whether Peter was fishing or, later, following Jesus as his disciple, he was always passionate. After being filled with the Holy Spirit at Pentecost, he boldly preached in Jerusalem and became a founding apostle of the early church (see Acts 2:1–41). By the time Peter wrote this letter, the gospel had reached Rome and far beyond, and believers had been scattered due to opposition and violent persecution. In this first section of his letter, he acknowledges the trials his readers are facing but reminds them they have a precious salvation in Christ that gives them hope and joy. This is an inheritance from God witnessed by the Old Testament prophets that will never fade—and it is one even desired by the angels in heaven!

OBSERVATION

*Read 1 Peter 1:1–12 from the New International
Version or the New King James Version.*

NEW INTERNATIONAL VERSION

¹ Peter, an apostle of Jesus Christ,

To God's elect, exiles scattered throughout the provinces of Pontus, Galatia, Cappadocia, Asia and Bithynia, ² who have been chosen according to the foreknowledge of God the Father, through the sanctifying work of the Spirit, to be obedient to Jesus Christ and sprinkled with his blood:

Grace and peace be yours in abundance.

³ Praise be to the God and Father of our Lord Jesus Christ! In his great mercy he has given us new birth into a living hope through the resurrection of Jesus Christ from the dead, ⁴ and into an inheritance that can never perish, spoil or fade. This inheritance is kept in heaven for you, ⁵ who through faith are shielded by God's power until the coming of the salvation that is ready to be revealed in the last time. ⁶ In all this you greatly rejoice, though now for a little while you may have had to suffer grief in all kinds of trials. ⁷ These have come so that the proven genuineness of your faith—of greater worth than gold, which perishes even though refined by fire—may result in praise, glory and honor when Jesus Christ is revealed. ⁸ Though you have not seen him, you love him; and even though you do not see him now, you believe in him and are filled with an inexpressible and glorious joy, ⁹ for you are receiving the end result of your faith, the salvation of your souls.

¹⁰ Concerning this salvation, the prophets, who spoke of the grace that was to come to you, searched intently and with the greatest care, ¹¹ trying to find out the time and circumstances to which the Spirit of Christ in them was pointing when he predicted the sufferings of the Messiah and the glories that would follow. ¹² It was revealed to them that they were not serving themselves but you, when they spoke of the things

that have now been told you by those who have preached the gospel to you by the Holy Spirit sent from heaven. Even angels long to look into these things.

NEW KING JAMES VERSION

[1] Peter, an apostle of Jesus Christ,

To the pilgrims of the Dispersion in Pontus, Galatia, Cappadocia, Asia, and Bithynia, [2] elect according to the foreknowledge of God the Father, in sanctification of the Spirit, for obedience and sprinkling of the blood of Jesus Christ:

Grace to you and peace be multiplied.

[3] Blessed be the God and Father of our Lord Jesus Christ, who according to His abundant mercy has begotten us again to a living hope through the resurrection of Jesus Christ from the dead, [4] to an inheritance incorruptible and undefiled and that does not fade away, reserved in heaven for you, [5] who are kept by the power of God through faith for salvation ready to be revealed in the last time.

[6] In this you greatly rejoice, though now for a little while, if need be, you have been grieved by various trials, [7] that the genuineness of your faith, being much more precious than gold that perishes, though it is tested by fire, may be found to praise, honor, and glory at the revelation of Jesus Christ, [8] whom having not seen you love. Though now you do not see Him, yet believing, you rejoice with joy inexpressible and full of glory, [9] receiving the end of your faith—the salvation of your souls.

[10] Of this salvation the prophets have inquired and searched carefully, who prophesied of the grace that would come to you, [11] searching what, or what manner of time, the Spirit of Christ who was in them was indicating when He testified beforehand the sufferings of Christ and the glories that would follow. [12] To them it was revealed that, not to themselves, but to us they were ministering the things which now have been reported to you through those who have preached the gospel to you by the Holy Spirit sent from heaven—things which angels desire to look into.

EXPLORATION

1. How does Peter describe the recipients of this letter?

2. What does it mean that God plans to make you *holy*? How does he accomplish this?

3. What is the inheritance you have been given? How would you describe it?

4. How does Peter describe a "pure" or "genuine" faith in this passage?

5. How can your hope in Jesus help you to endure trials?

_____

_____

_____

_____

6. In what ways have the trials in your life strengthened your faith?

_____

_____

_____

_____

INSPIRATION

There is something about a living testimony that gives us courage. Once we see someone else emerging from life's dark tunnels, we realize that we, too, can overcome.

Could this be why Jesus is called our pioneer? Is this one of the reasons that he consented to enter the horrid chambers of death? It must be. His words, though persuasive, were not enough. His promises, though true, didn't quite allay the fear of the people. His actions, even the act of calling Lazarus from the tomb, didn't convince the crowds that death was nothing to fear.

No. In the eyes of humanity, death was still the black veil that separated them from joy. There was no victory over this hooded foe. Its putrid odor invaded the nostrils of every human, convincing them that life was only meant to end abruptly and senselessly.

It was left to the Son of God to disclose the true nature of this force. It was on the cross that the showdown occurred. Christ called for Satan's cards. Weary of seeing humanity fooled by a coverup, he entered the tunnel of death to prove that there was indeed an exit. And, as the world darkened, creation held her breath.

Satan threw his best punch, but it wasn't enough. Even the darkness of hell's tunnel was no match for God's Son. Even the chambers of Hades couldn't stop this raider. Legions of screaming demons held nothing over the Lion of Judah.

Christ emerged from death's tunnel, lifted a triumphant fist toward the sky, and freed all from the fear of death. (From *Shaped by God* by Max Lucado.)

REACTION

7. What are some of the ways that Jesus offers you a living hope in your life?

_____

_____

_____

_____

8. How would your life be different if you did not have this living hope?

_____

_____

_____

_____

9. In what way does your hope for the future change the way you live each day?

_____

_____

_____

_____

10. What does it mean to rejoice in your salvation?

_____

_____

_____

_____

11. How do Peter's words in this passage affect your attitude toward the trials in your life?

_____

_____

_____

_____

12. What do want to remember from this passage the next time you face trials?

_____

_____

_____

_____

LIFE LESSONS

Peter not only describes a hopeful life in this passage but he also demonstrates one. He speaks to his readers as if they are already doing what they need to do in their circumstances—trusting fully in God in the midst of their trials and difficulties. His hope for them is unconditional. We will always face trouble, but we can face them assured the Lord is with us and that he will see to it his purposes are accomplished in us. That is hopeful living!

DEVOTION

Father, help us to see the joy that is before us. You have given us such a great treasure and inheritance—the promise of salvation. Forgive us for losing sight of our glorious future. Renew our vision and help us strain toward the goal of our faith—the salvation of our souls. And when we face trials, remind us that you have won the ultimate victory.

JOURNALING

What are the blessings in your life that God has given to you?

FOR FURTHER READING

To complete the books of 1 and 2 Peter during this twelve-part study, read 1 Peter 1:1–12. For more Bible passages on hope, read Psalm 42:5; Proverbs 23:17–18; Jeremiah 29:11; Romans 8:24–25; 1 Corinthians 15:19–32; 1 Thessalonians 1:3; Titus 1:2; 2:11–13; and Hebrews 10:23.

NEW LIFE IN CHRIST

*For you have been born again, not of
perishable seed, but of imperishable, through
the living and enduring word of God.*
1 PETER 1:23

REFLECTION

Think of your lifestyle before you became a follower of Christ. Think about some of the issues you were facing that first drove you to seriously consider accepting Jesus as your Savior. How is your life different now? In what ways is it the same?

_____

_____

_____

_____

_____

SITUATION

Peter wrote his first letter to group of believers who were enduring great persecution and difficult times. He wanted to point them to the hope they had in Christ—a hope they could focus on in the midst of their trials. In this next section of his letter, he continues to show his readers how they are to set their minds on this greater hope and walk in this new life that they have been given. He encourages them to not cling to their former ways or to the material things of this world—which he knows are fleeting and soon pass away. Instead, they are to pursue a life of holiness, reverence toward God, and genuine love toward their fellow believers.

OBSERVATION

Read 1 Peter 1:13–25 from the New International Version or the New King James Version.

NEW INTERNATIONAL VERSION

¹³ Therefore, with minds that are alert and fully sober, set your hope on the grace to be brought to you when Jesus Christ is revealed at his

coming. ¹⁴ As obedient children, do not conform to the evil desires you had when you lived in ignorance. ¹⁵ But just as he who called you is holy, so be holy in all you do; ¹⁶ for it is written: "Be holy, because I am holy."

¹⁷ Since you call on a Father who judges each person's work impartially, live out your time as foreigners here in reverent fear. ¹⁸ For you know that it was not with perishable things such as silver or gold that you were redeemed from the empty way of life handed down to you from your ancestors, ¹⁹ but with the precious blood of Christ, a lamb without blemish or defect. ²⁰ He was chosen before the creation of the world, but was revealed in these last times for your sake. ²¹ Through him you believe in God, who raised him from the dead and glorified him, and so your faith and hope are in God.

²² Now that you have purified yourselves by obeying the truth so that you have sincere love for each other, love one another deeply, from the heart. ²³ For you have been born again, not of perishable seed, but of imperishable, through the living and enduring word of God. ²⁴ For,

> "All people are like grass,
>   and all their glory is like the flowers of the field;
> the grass withers and the flowers fall,
>   ²⁵ but the word of the Lord endures forever."

And this is the word that was preached to you.

NEW KING JAMES VERSION

¹³ Therefore gird up the loins of your mind, be sober, and rest your hope fully upon the grace that is to be brought to you at the revelation of Jesus Christ; ¹⁴ as obedient children, not conforming yourselves to the former lusts, as in your ignorance; ¹⁵ but as He who called you is holy, you also be holy in all your conduct, ¹⁶ because it is written, "Be holy, for I am holy."

¹⁷ And if you call on the Father, who without partiality judges according to each one's work, conduct yourselves throughout the time of your stay here in fear; ¹⁸ knowing that you were not redeemed with corruptible

things, like silver or gold, from your aimless conduct received by tradition from your fathers, ¹⁹ but with the precious blood of Christ, as of a lamb without blemish and without spot. ²⁰ He indeed was foreordained before the foundation of the world, but was manifest in these last times for you ²¹ who through Him believe in God, who raised Him from the dead and gave Him glory, so that your faith and hope are in God.

²² Since you have purified your souls in obeying the truth through the Spirit in sincere love of the brethren, love one another fervently with a pure heart, ²³ having been born again, not of corruptible seed but incorruptible, through the word of God which lives and abides forever, ²⁴ because

"All flesh is as grass,
And all the glory of man as the flower of the grass.
The grass withers,
And its flower falls away,
²⁵ But the word of the LORD endures forever."

Now this is the word which by the gospel was preached to you.

EXPLORATION

1. How does Peter say your life should change after you accept Jesus as your Savior?

_____

_____

_____

_____

2. What does it mean to be *holy*? How would you define this word?

_____

_____

3. What does it mean to "live out your time as foreigners" on this earth?

_____

_____

_____

4. How does Peter say you were redeemed? How does this affect the way you live?

_____

_____

_____

5. Why is it important to understand the price Jesus paid for your salvation?

_____

_____

_____

6. Peter says that being pure enables you to demonstrate true love to others. What is the relationship between being pure and showing love?

_____

_____

_____

INSPIRATION

Most of us had a hard time learning to tie our shoes. Squirting toothpaste on a brush was tough enough, but tightening shoes by wrapping strings together?

Nothing easy about that. Besides, who needs them? Wear loafers. Go barefoot. Who came up with the idea of shoes anyhow?

And knees don't help. Always in your face. Leaning around them, pushing them away—a person can't concentrate.

And, oh, the advice! Everyone had a different approach. "Make a tree with the loop, and let the squirrel run around it into the hole." "Shape a rabbit ear, and then wrap it with a ribbon." Dad said, "Go fast." Your uncle said to take your time. Can't anyone agree? Only on one thing. You need to know how.

Learning to tie your shoes is a rite of passage. Right in there with first grade and first bike is first shoe tying. But, oh, how dreadful is the process.

Just when you think you've made the loops and circled the tree . . . you get the rabbit ears in either hand and give them a triumphant yank and, voila!—a knot. Unbeknownst to you, you've just been inducted into reality.

My friend Roy used to sit on a park bench for a few minutes each morning. He liked to watch the kids gather and play at the bus stop. One day he noticed a little fellow, maybe five or six years of age, struggling to board the bus. While others were climbing on, he was leaning down, frantically trying to disentangle a knotted shoestring. He grew more anxious by the moment, frantic eyes darting back and forth between the shoe and the ride.

All of a sudden it was too late. The door closed.

The boy fell back on his haunches and sighed. That's when he saw Roy. With tear-filled eyes he looked at the man on the bench and asked, "Do you untie knots?"

Jesus loves that request.

Life gets tangled. People mess up. You never outgrow the urge to look up and say, "Help!"

Jesus had a way of appearing at such moments. Peter's empty boat. Nicodemus' empty heart. Matthew has a friend issue. A woman has a health issue. Look who shows up.

Jesus, our next door Savior. "Do you untie knots?"

"Yes." (From *Next Door Savior* by Max Lucado.)

REACTION

7. How does this illustration of shoe-tying and tangled laces help you relate to Peter's words about being obedient, holy, and pure?

8. How would you explain what it means to be *redeemed* to a friend with no religious background?

9. Who helped you realize your need for a spiritual transformation that only God could accomplish?

10. In what ways do believers sometimes trivialize Christ's sacrifice?

11. Why is it often so difficult to change your ways even after you are born again?

_____

_____

_____

_____

12. What old habits have you needed God's help to give up? How has he accomplished those changes in your life?

_____

_____

_____

_____

LIFE LESSONS

We have been charged to "gird up the loins of [our] mind" (1 Peter 1:13 NKJV) and make sure our spiritual shoelaces have been tied. The Christian life involves action, intention, and obedience. We must not rely on those things that wither and fade but only on what God tells us in his Word. The way we live each day demonstrates how we value what Jesus has done for us.

DEVOTION

Father, we thank you for the gift of grace that is ours through Jesus Christ. We claim your salvation and ask you to help us respond with humility and obedience. Father, you have commanded us to be holy, just as you are holy. But we can do nothing without you. So we ask you to work through us, by your Spirit, and transform us into your likeness.

JOURNALING

What evidence of new life in Christ can you see in yourself?

FOR FURTHER READING

To complete the books of 1 and 2 Peter during this twelve-part study, read 1 Peter 1:13–25. For more Bible passages on spiritual rebirth, read John 3:3–8; 2 Corinthians 5:17; Galatians 6:15; Ephesians 2:4–10; Titus 3:3–7; 1 Peter 1:3; and 1 John 3:9.

THE CORNERSTONE

Coming to Him as to a living stone, rejected indeed by men, but chosen by God and precious, you also, as living stones, are being built up a spiritual house, a holy priesthood, to offer up spiritual sacrifices acceptable to God through Jesus Christ.
1 PETER 2:4–5 NKJV

REFLECTION

Bring up the name of *Jesus* in a conversation, and you're likely to get some strong reactions. What are some typical things you've heard people say about Jesus? Why do you think people in this world either *hate* and *ignore* him or *love* and *follow* him?

_____

_____

_____

_____

_____

_____

_____

_____

_____

_____

SITUATION

When Jesus gave Peter his new name, he said to him, "You are Peter, and on this rock I will build my church, and the gates of Hades will not overcome it" (Matthew 16:18). The image of *stone* brings to mind the firm foundation and source of strength that believers have in Christ—a foundation that will not fail even in the midst of the worst storms. Peter goes on to note that Jesus, like a stone mason, is continually crafting his followers into a "spiritual house" and holy priesthood. Yet this requires action on our part, for we need to crave the Word of God and desire "pure spiritual milk" (1 Peter 2:2) so that we will grow strong in our faith.

OBSERVATION

*Read 1 Peter 2:1–10 from the New International
Version or the New King James Version.*

New International Version

[1] Therefore, rid yourselves of all malice and all deceit, hypocrisy, envy, and slander of every kind. [2] Like newborn babies, crave pure spiritual milk, so that by it you may grow up in your salvation, [3] now that you have tasted that the Lord is good.

[4] As you come to him, the living Stone—rejected by humans but chosen by God and precious to him— [5] you also, like living stones, are being built into a spiritual house to be a holy priesthood, offering spiritual sacrifices acceptable to God through Jesus Christ. [6] For in Scripture it says:

> "See, I lay a stone in Zion,
>   a chosen and precious cornerstone,
> and the one who trusts in him
>   will never be put to shame."

[7] Now to you who believe, this stone is precious. But to those who do not believe,

> "The stone the builders rejected
>   has become the cornerstone,"

[8] and,

> "A stone that causes people to stumble
>   and a rock that makes them fall."

They stumble because they disobey the message—which is also what they were destined for.

⁹ But you are a chosen people, a royal priesthood, a holy nation, God's special possession, that you may declare the praises of him who called you out of darkness into his wonderful light. ¹⁰ Once you were not a people, but now you are the people of God; once you had not received mercy, but now you have received mercy.

NEW KING JAMES VERSION

¹ Therefore, laying aside all malice, all deceit, hypocrisy, envy, and all evil speaking, ² as newborn babes, desire the pure milk of the word, that you may grow thereby, ³ if indeed you have tasted that the Lord is gracious.

⁴ Coming to Him as to a living stone, rejected indeed by men, but chosen by God and precious, ⁵ you also, as living stones, are being built up a spiritual house, a holy priesthood, to offer up spiritual sacrifices acceptable to God through Jesus Christ. ⁶ Therefore it is also contained in the Scripture,

> "Behold, I lay in Zion
> A chief cornerstone, elect, precious,
> And he who believes on Him will by no means be put to shame."

⁷ Therefore, to you who believe, He is precious; but to those who are disobedient,

> "The stone which the builders rejected
> Has become the chief cornerstone,"

⁸ and

> "A stone of stumbling
> And a rock of offense."

They stumble, being disobedient to the word, to which they also were appointed.

⁹ But you are a chosen generation, a royal priesthood, a holy nation, His own special people, that you may proclaim the praises of Him who called you out of darkness into His marvelous light; ¹⁰ who once were not a people but are now the people of God, who had not obtained mercy but now have obtained mercy.

EXPLORATION

1. What are some of the attitudes and behaviors that Peter calls you to remove from your life?

_____

_____

_____

_____

_____

2. What does it mean to "crave spiritual milk" (verse 2)? How does that relate to your spiritual growth in Christ?

_____

_____

_____

_____

_____

3. Why does Peter say that believers in Christ are "living stones" (verse 5)? What positive traits is Peter calling you to exhibit by using that term?

_____

_____

_____

_____

4. What promise is given for those who choose to trust in Jesus as the cornerstone?

_____

_____

_____

_____

5. What does Peter mean when he says Jesus as the cornerstone causes some to stumble?

_____

_____

_____

_____

6. What special role has God given to you because you are a follower of Christ?

_____

_____

_____

INSPIRATION

When times get hard, remember Jesus. When people don't listen, remember Jesus. When tears come, remember Jesus. When disappointment is your bed partner, remember Jesus. When fear pitches his tent in your front yard. When death looms, when anger singes, when shame weighs heavily. Remember Jesus. . . .

Can you still remember? Are you still in love with Him? . . . Remember Jesus. Before you remember anything, remember Him. If you forget anything, don't forget Him.

Oh, but how quickly we forget. So much happens through the years. So many changes within. So many alterations without. And, somewhere, back there, we leave him. We don't turn away from him . . . we just don't take him with us. Assignments come. Promotions come. Budgets are made. Kids are born, and the Christ . . . the Christ is forgotten.

Has it been a while since you stared at the heavens in speechless amazement? Has it been a while since you realized God's divinity and your carnality?

If it has, then you need to know something. He is still there. He hasn't left. Under all those papers and books and reports and years. In the midst of all those voices and faces and memories and pictures, He is still there.

Do yourself a favor. Stand before him again. Or, better, allow him to stand before you. Go into your upper room and wait. Wait until he comes. And when he appears, don't leave. Run your fingers over his feet. Place your hand in the pierced side. And look into those eyes. Those same eyes that melted the gates of hell and sent the demons scurrying and Satan running. Look at them as they look at you. You'll never be the same. (From *Six Hours One Friday* by Max Lucado.)

REACTION

7. Think about the enthusiasm and commitment you had for Christ when you first became his follower. Why is that level of enthusiasm and commitment difficult to maintain?

_____

_____

_____

_____

8. What does it mean to truly make Jesus the *cornerstone* on which your life is built?

_____

_____

_____

_____

9. How has Jesus, as the cornerstone, defined the shape of your life?

_____

_____

_____

10. Peter states that believers in Christ "are a chosen people, a royal priesthood, a holy nation" (verse 9). Does that match up with how you tend to view yourself? Why or why not?

_____

_____

_____

11. How do Peter's words in this passage reaffirm your sense of worth and value in God's eyes?

_____

_____

_____

12. What are some ways you can help others not to stumble when it comes to obeying the message of Christ?

_____

_____

_____

LIFE LESSONS

The purpose of the cornerstone in a building is to establish the lines. This rock has to be square and plumb, because the rest of the building takes its cues from the first block. Jesus may be a stumbling block for those who don't believe, but for us, he serves as the solid base for our lives. If we try to construct our lives without him, we will fail. But if our lives are anchored to him and oriented to him, the winds and storms of life will not destroy what we've built. All the other complimentary terms used to describe us in this passage relate directly to our relationship with Jesus. We are called these names because of him and what he has done for us.

DEVOTION

God, forgive us for the times we have left you behind in our struggle to get ahead. Forgive us for forgetting who you are and what you have done for us. We know you have been there—always waiting, always hoping, and always ready to forgive. May we understand what it means to make you the cornerstone of our lives.

JOURNALING

How would you compare your commitment to Christ when you first believed to your commitment to him now?

FOR FURTHER READING

To complete the books of 1 and 2 Peter during this twelve-part study, read 1 Peter 2:1–10. For more Bible passages on Christ the cornerstone, read Psalm 118:21–24; Isaiah 28:16–18; Zechariah 10:4; Matthew 21:42–43; Acts 4:10–12; Romans 9:33; 1 Corinthians 3:10–13; and Ephesians 2:19–22.

FOLLOWING JESUS' EXAMPLE

To this you were called, because Christ suffered for you, leaving you an example, that you should follow in his steps.
1 PETER 2:21

REFLECTION

Some people challenge us, by the very quality of the way they lead their lives, to be more like then. Think of a fellow believer whom you greatly admire. In what ways does that person's life challenge you? How would you like to better model your life after that person's example?

_____

_____

_____

_____

_____

SITUATION

Christianity had swept like wildfire through the ranks of the upper/ middle class and slaves alike in the Roman Empire. Yet the growth of the movement did not come without persecution and suffering for these believers at the hands of those who did not accept Jesus and follow his ways. In this section, Peter reminds his readers that they are actually "foreigners and exiles" in this world (2:11), and as such they are to abstain from sin, submit to God (and the authorities he has put in place), and continually look to Christ as the example for right living.

OBSERVATION

Read 1 Peter 2:11–25 from the New International
Version or the New King James Version.

NEW INTERNATIONAL VERSION

[11] Dear friends, I urge you, as foreigners and exiles, to abstain from sinful desires, which wage war against your soul. [12] Live such good lives among

the pagans that, though they accuse you of doing wrong, they may see your good deeds and glorify God on the day he visits us.

[13] Submit yourselves for the Lord's sake to every human authority: whether to the emperor, as the supreme authority, [14] or to governors, who are sent by him to punish those who do wrong and to commend those who do right. [15] For it is God's will that by doing good you should silence the ignorant talk of foolish people.[16] Live as free people, but do not use your freedom as a cover-up for evil; live as God's slaves. [17] Show proper respect to everyone, love the family of believers, fear God, honor the emperor.

[18] Slaves, in reverent fear of God submit yourselves to your masters, not only to those who are good and considerate, but also to those who are harsh. [19] For it is commendable if someone bears up under the pain of unjust suffering because they are conscious of God. [20] But how is it to your credit if you receive a beating for doing wrong and endure it? But if you suffer for doing good and you endure it, this is commendable before God. [21] To this you were called, because Christ suffered for you, leaving you an example, that you should follow in his steps.

> [22] "He committed no sin,
>   and no deceit was found in his mouth."

[23] When they hurled their insults at him, he did not retaliate; when he suffered, he made no threats. Instead, he entrusted himself to him who judges justly. [24] "He himself bore our sins" in his body on the cross, so that we might die to sins and live for righteousness; "by his wounds you have been healed." [25] For "you were like sheep going astray," but now you have returned to the Shepherd and Overseer of your souls.

New King James Version

[11] Beloved, I beg you as sojourners and pilgrims, abstain from fleshly lusts which war against the soul, [12] having your conduct honorable among the Gentiles, that when they speak against you as evildoers, they may, by your good works which they observe, glorify God in the day of visitation.

¹³ Therefore submit yourselves to every ordinance of man for the Lord's sake, whether to the king as supreme, ¹⁴ or to governors, as to those who are sent by him for the punishment of evildoers and for the praise of those who do good. ¹⁵ For this is the will of God, that by doing good you may put to silence the ignorance of foolish men— ¹⁶ as free, yet not using liberty as a cloak for vice, but as bondservants of God. ¹⁷ Honor all people. Love the brotherhood. Fear God. Honor the king.

¹⁸ Servants, be submissive to your masters with all fear, not only to the good and gentle, but also to the harsh. ¹⁹ For this is commendable, if because of conscience toward God one endures grief, suffering wrongfully. ²⁰ For what credit is it if, when you are beaten for your faults, you take it patiently? But when you do good and suffer, if you take it patiently, this is commendable before God. ²¹ For to this you were called, because Christ also suffered for us, leaving us an example, that you should follow His steps:

²² "Who committed no sin,
Nor was deceit found in His mouth";

²³ who, when He was reviled, did not revile in return; when He suffered, He did not threaten, but committed Himself to Him who judges righteously; ²⁴ who Himself bore our sins in His own body on the tree, that we, having died to sins, might live for righteousness—by whose stripes you were healed. ²⁵ For you were like sheep going astray, but have now returned to the Shepherd and Overseer of your souls.

EXPLORATION

1. How do sinful desires "wage war against your soul" (verse 11)?

_____

_____

_____

_____

2. Why is it important for you to lead a godly life even in difficult circumstances?

3. Why does Peter say you should yield to human authorities?

4. What happens when believers endure suffering for doing good?

5. What can we learn from Jesus about responding to unfair treatment?

6. What was the result of Jesus' willingness to endure suffering, scorn, and death on the cross?

INSPIRATION

As believers in Christ, how are we to respond when the boss makes snide comments about us? When others talk bad about us? When people just irritate us?

Peter suggests we look to the example of Christ. "When they hurled their insults at him, he did not retaliate; when he suffered, he made no threats. Instead, he entrusted himself to him who judges justly" (1 Peter 2:23).

Jesus, after hours of put-downs, mockings, and parodies, said nothing. He did not fire back with one sarcastic atomic bomb. And you would have to think, with his mastery of the language and the number of clever verbal assaults he'd heard in his lifetime, he could have made them sweat.

So what are we supposed to do when people hurl insults at us?

Did you see what Jesus did *not* do when the crowds and the guards insulted him? He did not retaliate. He did not bite back. He did not say, "I'll get you!" No, these statements were not found on Christ's lips.

Did you see what Jesus *did* do? He prayed. He "entrusted himself to him who judges justly." Or, said more simply, he left the judging to God. He did not take on the task of seeking revenge. He demanded no apology. He hired no bounty hunters.

Never, never have I seen such love. If ever a person deserved a shot at revenge and had the power to do some serious supernatural damage in the process, Jesus did. But he didn't call down armies. He called down grace. He died for them.

How could he do it? I don't know. But I do know that all of a sudden my wounds seem painless. My grudges and hard feelings are quite petty.

Days later, Jesus rose again, victorious, to eternal life, while the mockers woke up still stewing in their miserable lives—angry, painful, unforgiven, graceless. In the end, truth won out. It always does. (Adapted from *Max on Life* by Max Lucado.)

REACTION

7. How do you tend to react when others talk bad about you, hurt you, or mistreat you?

8. Why do you think Jesus chose not to retaliate against his attackers— even though he could have surely put them all in their place?

9. In what way does Christ's example affect the way you are viewing your problems and pain?

10. In what circumstances is it tempting to retaliate?

11. When has God helped you forgive someone who hurt you deeply?

_____

_____

_____

_____

12. How can you fight the urge to get back at people who mistreat you?

_____

_____

_____

_____

LIFE LESSONS

Following Jesus' example when responding to mistreatment can seriously cramp our style. The problem isn't with Jesus' worthiness as an example, or the importance of following him, but that our "style" is made up of selfishness, pride, and personal agendas. In the laboratory of life, God wants to produce Jesus' character in us. In order to do so, he's not nearly as concerned with what happens to us as with how we respond. Following Jesus' example will take everything we have.

DEVOTION

Father, sometimes the urge to seek revenge seems too strong to resist. Even though we have experienced your great mercy and love, we refuse to extend your grace to others. Forgive us, Father, for choosing to retaliate instead of forgive. Remind us of how Jesus dealt with injustice and unfairness when he was on earth, and give us the strength to follow his example.

JOURNALING

Whom do you need to forgive? How can you follow Jesus' example of love in that relationship?

FOR FURTHER READING

To complete the books of 1 and 2 Peter during this twelve-part study, read 1 Peter 2:11–25. For more Bible passages on following Jesus' example, read Matthew 16:24–27; John 8:12; 12:26; 13:15; 1 Corinthians 11:1; Galatians 5:16–18; Ephesians 5:1–2; and 1 Thessalonians 1:4–6.

LESSON FIVE

HOLY LIVING

*Do not let your adornment be merely outward . . .
rather let it be the hidden person of the heart, with
the incorruptible beauty of a gentle and quiet spirit,
which is very precious in the sight of God.*
1 PETER 3:3–4 NKJV

REFLECTION

In this passage, Peter talks about living from the inside out. Consider someone you know who displays inner strength or inner beauty. How would you define those traits? What habits or disciplines do you think help develop a person's inner strength and beauty?

SITUATION

Peter now follows up the general points he has made about submitting to Christ, showing respect to those in authority, and following the Lord's example with some practical teaching on the topic of marriage. He notes that just as believers are to submit to Christ, wives are to submit to their husbands (even if they are non-believers)—but husbands, in same way, are to show respect by dwelling "with them with understanding" (3:7) and giving them honor. Peter's words reveal that the depth of our commitment to following Jesus isn't measured by how we perform in casual exchanges with people but by how that commitment affects our *central* relationships. In other words, does Jesus have the last word on how we treat our spouse?

OBSERVATION

*Read 1 Peter 3:1–7 from the New International
Version or the New King James Version.*

NEW INTERNATIONAL VERSION

[1] Wives, in the same way submit yourselves to your own husbands so that, if any of them do not believe the word, they may be won over without words by the behavior of their wives, [2] when they see the purity and reverence of your lives. [3] Your beauty should not come from outward adornment, such as elaborate hairstyles and the wearing of gold jewelry or fine clothes. [4] Rather, it should be that of your inner self, the unfading beauty of a gentle and quiet spirit, which is of great worth in God's sight. [5] For this is the way the holy women of the past who put their hope in God used to adorn themselves. They submitted themselves to their own husbands, [6] like Sarah, who obeyed Abraham and called him her lord. You are her daughters if you do what is right and do not give way to fear.

[7] Husbands, in the same way be considerate as you live with your wives, and treat them with respect as the weaker partner and as heirs with you of the gracious gift of life, so that nothing will hinder your prayers.

NEW KING JAMES VERSION

[1] Wives, likewise, be submissive to your own husbands, that even if some do not obey the word, they, without a word, may be won by the conduct of their wives, [2] when they observe your chaste conduct accompanied by fear. [3] Do not let your adornment be merely outward—arranging the hair, wearing gold, or putting on fine apparel— [4] rather let it be the hidden person of the heart, with the incorruptible beauty of a gentle and quiet spirit, which is very precious in the sight of God. [5] For in this manner, in former times, the holy women who trusted in God also adorned themselves, being submissive to their own husbands, [6] as Sarah obeyed Abraham, calling him lord, whose daughters you are if you do good and are not afraid with any terror.

⁷ Husbands, likewise, dwell with them with understanding, giving honor to the wife, as to the weaker vessel, and as being heirs together of the grace of life, that your prayers may not be hindered.

EXPLORATION

1. How does Peter say believing wives can win their unbelieving husbands to Christ?

_____

_____

_____

_____

_____

_____

2. Why is inner beauty precious to God?

_____

_____

_____

_____

_____

_____

3. What are some ways to cultivate inner beauty?

_____

_____

_____

_____

_____

4. What can you learn from the example of women in the Bible like Sarah?

5. How does Peter say husbands are to treat their wives?

6. In what ways do others benefit when believers are considerate to one another and lead holy and pure lives?

INSPIRATION

Would you do what Jesus did? He swapped a spotless castle for a grimy stable. He exchanged the worship of angels for the company of killers. He could hold the universe in his palm but gave it up to float in the womb of a maiden.

If you were God, would you sleep on straw, nurse from a breast, and be clothed in a diaper? I wouldn't, but Christ did.

If you knew that only a few would care that you came, would you still come? If you knew that those you loved would laugh in your face, would you still care? If you knew that the tongues you made would mock you, the mouths you made would spit at you, the hands you made would crucify you, would you still make them? Christ did. Would you regard the immobile and invalid more important than yourself? Jesus did.

He humbled himself. He went from commanding angels to sleeping in the straw. From holding stars to clutching Mary's finger. The palm that held the universe took the nail of a soldier.

Why? Because that's what love does. It puts the beloved before itself. Your soul was more important than his blood. Your eternal life was more important than his earthly life. Your place in heaven was more important to him than his place in heaven, so he gave up his so you could have yours. He loves you that much, and because he loves you, you are of prime importance to him . . .

God notices the sparrows. He makes time for the children and takes note of the lepers. He offers the woman in adultery a second chance and the thief on the cross a personal invitation. Christ is partial to the beat up and done in and urges us to follow suit. "When you give a banquet, invite the poor, the crippled, the lame, the blind" (Luke 14:13).

Want to love others as God has loved you? Come thirsty. Drink deeply of God's love for you, and ask him to fill your heart with a love worth giving. (From *A Love Worth Giving* by Max Lucado.)

REACTION

7. What does Jesus' example teach you about humility and submitting your will to God?

_____

_____

_____

_____

_____

_____

8. What are some ways couples demonstrate humility and love in their marriage?

_____

_____

_____

_____

_____

_____

9. What are some ways couples demonstrate consideration and respect in their marriage?

_____

_____

_____

_____

_____

_____

10. Why is it important to realize becoming holy is a *process* and not a one-time event?

_____

_____

_____

_____

11. What is God's part and what is our responsibility in the sanctification process?

_____

_____

_____

_____

12. What about your life does Peter say will attract people to Christ?

_____

_____

_____

LIFE LESSONS

The word *crucible* carries a double meaning. It is a container designed to take the extreme heat of molten metal. It is also used to describe a severe test. Marriage functions like a relationship crucible. The wedding vows create a container for the high temperatures of relationship development. The holy lives that God wants in his children can be developed in the crucible of marriage, but the process isn't easy. It requires commitment, forgiveness, submission (to God and one another), and continued faithfulness through heat and cool. Yet the results are worth the efforts required!

DEVOTION

Father, we want to be holy, but we are weak and prone to sin. Manifest your holiness in us, especially in our closest relationships. Help us to surrender our selfish desires to your perfect will. Teach us what it means to live by your Spirit, not our flesh. Persuade others to believe in you through the example we set in our lives.

JOURNALING

What are some things in your life that you need to humbly submit to God?

FOR FURTHER READING

To complete the books of 1 and 2 Peter during this twelve-part study, read 1 Peter 3:1–7. For more Bible passages on holy living, read Leviticus 11:44–45; Romans 12:1–2; 1 Corinthians 1:2, 30; 1 Thessalonians 4:3–7; 2 Timothy 1:8–9; James 4:13–17; and Hebrews 10:10–14.

LOVING PEOPLE

Finally, all of you, be like-minded,
be sympathetic, love one another, be
compassionate and humble. Do not
repay evil or evil or insult with insult.
1 PETER 3:8–9

REFLECTION

Think about a time when someone demonstrated Christ's love to you in a practical way. What do you think it cost the person to help you? In what ways has that person's gesture affected the way you notice and respond to other people's needs?

_____

_____

_____

_____

_____

_____

_____

_____

_____

SITUATION

Peter understood that many of his readers were enduring trials and persecution simply for *being* Christians. However, it was something else entirely to suffer for *living* like a Christian in front of a world that was often hostile to the gospel. In this section, Peter calls on believers to not only do good in the midst of their suffering—and thus model the example of Christ to others—but to also be prepared to explain the hope of Jesus to others. To a watching world, the perseverance of a Christian in the face of persecution would have caused much curiosity. Peter wanted believers to be prepared to "give an answer to everyone who asks you to give the reason for the hope you have" (3:15), and in this way draw others into the family of God.

OBSERVATION

*Read 1 Peter 3:8–22 from the New International
Version or the New King James Version.*

New International Version

[8] Finally, all of you, be like-minded, be sympathetic, love one another, be compassionate and humble. [9] Do not repay evil with evil or insult with insult. On the contrary, repay evil with blessing, because to this you were called so that you may inherit a blessing. [10] For,

"Whoever would love life
   and see good days
must keep their tongue from evil
   and their lips from deceitful speech.
[11] They must turn from evil and do good;
   they must seek peace and pursue it.
[12] For the eyes of the Lord are on the righteous
   and his ears are attentive to their prayer,
but the face of the Lord is against those who do evil."

[13] Who is going to harm you if you are eager to do good? [14] But even if you should suffer for what is right, you are blessed. "Do not fear their threats; do not be frightened." [15] But in your hearts revere Christ as Lord. Always be prepared to give an answer to everyone who asks you to give the reason for the hope that you have. But do this with gentleness and respect, [16] keeping a clear conscience, so that those who speak maliciously against your good behavior in Christ may be ashamed of their slander. [17] For it is better, if it is God's will, to suffer for doing good than for doing evil. [18] For Christ also suffered once for sins, the righteous for the unrighteous, to bring you to God. He was put to death in the body but made alive in the Spirit. [19] After being made alive, he went and made proclamation to the imprisoned spirits— [20] to those who were

disobedient long ago when God waited patiently in the days of Noah while the ark was being built. In it only a few people, eight in all, were saved through water, [21] and this water symbolizes baptism that now saves you also—not the removal of dirt from the body but the pledge of a clear conscience toward God. It saves you by the resurrection of Jesus Christ, [22] who has gone into heaven and is at God's right hand—with angels, authorities and powers in submission to him.

New King James Version

[8] Finally, all of you be of one mind, having compassion for one another; love as brothers, be tenderhearted, be courteous; [9] not returning evil for evil or reviling for reviling, but on the contrary blessing, knowing that you were called to this, that you may inherit a blessing. [10] For

> "He who would love life
> And see good days,
> Let him refrain his tongue from evil,
> And his lips from speaking deceit.
> [11] Let him turn away from evil and do good;
> Let him seek peace and pursue it.
> [12] For the eyes of the Lord are on the righteous,
> And His ears are open to their prayers;
> But the face of the Lord is against those who do evil."

[13] And who is he who will harm you if you become followers of what is good? [14] But even if you should suffer for righteousness' sake, you are blessed. "And do not be afraid of their threats, nor be troubled." [15] But sanctify the Lord God in your hearts, and always be ready to give a defense to everyone who asks you a reason for the hope that is in you, with meekness and fear; [16] having a good conscience, that when they defame you as evildoers, those who revile your good conduct in Christ may be ashamed. [17] For it is better, if it is the will of God, to suffer for doing good than for doing evil.

[18] For Christ also suffered once for sins, the just for the unjust, that He might bring us to God, being put to death in the flesh but made alive by the Spirit, [19] by whom also He went and preached to the spirits in prison, [20] who formerly were disobedient, when once the Divine longsuffering waited in the days of Noah, while the ark was being prepared, in which a few, that is, eight souls, were saved through water. [21] There is also an antitype which now saves us—baptism (not the removal of the filth of the flesh, but the answer of a good conscience toward God), through the resurrection of Jesus Christ, [22] who has gone into heaven and is at the right hand of God, angels and authorities and powers having been made subject to Him.

EXPLORATION

1. How does Peter say that believers in Christ are to treat one another?

2. How has your church been an example of Christian behavior in the community?

3. When do you find it most difficult to demonstrate a loving attitude toward others?

4. Why is it important to "be prepared to give an answer" about the hope you have found in Christ (verse 15)? When have you been asked to offer this answer?

_____

_____

_____

_____

5. Why does Peter encourage you to respond with gentleness and respect to others—even if they are speaking maliciously about your behavior in Christ?

_____

_____

_____

_____

6. What difference should Christ's mercy toward you make in how you treat others?

_____

_____

_____

_____

INSPIRATION

In our house we called 5:00 PM the piranha hour. It was the time of day when everyone wanted a piece of Mom. Sara, the baby, was hungry. Andrea wanted Mom to read her a book. Jenna wanted help with her homework. And I—the ever-loving, ever sensitive husband—wanted Denalyn to drop everything and talk to me about my day.

When is your piranha hour? When do people in your world demand much and offer little?

Every boss has had a day in which the requests outnumber the results. There's not a businessperson alive who hasn't groaned as an armada of assignments docks at his or her desk. For the teacher, the piranha hour often begins when the first student enters and ends when the last student leaves.

Piranha hours. Parents have them, bosses endure them, secretaries dread them, teachers are besieged by them, and Jesus taught us how to live through them successfully.

When hands extended and voices demanded, Jesus responded with love. He did so because the code within him disarmed the alarm. The code is worth noting: "People are precious."

I can hear somebody raising an objection at this point. "Yes, but it was easier for Jesus. He was God. He could do more than I can. After all, he was divine."

True, Jesus was equally God and man. But don't be too quick to dismiss what he did. Consider his loving response from another angle.

Consider that, along with his holy strength, he also had a holy awareness. . . . Jesus knew the hearts of each person. He knew why they were there and what they would do. . . .

Don't be too quick to attribute Jesus' compassion to his divinity. Remember both sides. For each time Jesus healed, he had to overlook the future and the past.

Something, by the way, that he still does.

Have you noticed that God doesn't ask you to prove that you will put your salary to good use? Have you noticed that God doesn't turn off your oxygen supply when you misuse his gifts? Aren't you glad that God doesn't give you only that which you remember to thank him for? (Has it been a while since you thanked God for your spleen? Me too. But I still have one.)

God's goodness is spurred by his nature, not by our worthiness. (From *In the Eye of the Storm* by Max Lucado.)

REACTION

7. When is your "piranha hour"? What demands does this time bring?

8. How does Jesus' example demonstrate how to navigate "piranha hours"?

9. What are some ways you have found the strength to love people, even when they have nothing to give in return?

10. How do you respond to the idea that each time Jesus chose to heal a person, he had to overlook the future and the past?

11. In what ways can you remind yourself of Christ's example the next time you feel overwhelmed by the demands of others?

_____

_____

_____

_____

12. What practical steps can you take to promote better harmony in the body of Christ?

_____

_____

_____

_____

LIFE LESSONS

The Christian life is often counter to human instincts. In our natural state, we humans want to return evil for evil and reviling for reviling. We believe that what goes around comes around, and we want to give it an extra shove when it goes by us! However, if we're going to follow Jesus, we can't follow our natural instincts. If we are going to obey Jesus' command to love others, we have to ignore our inclination to have things our way. Jesus goes beyond his role as our example—he also empowers us to love beyond what we could ever do in our own strength.

DEVOTION

Father, when we feel incapable of showing your love to others, when we have nothing left to give, we pray you would fill us with your grace. During those dry, dark times, Father, we ask that you would give us the strength to love sacrificially. Teach us how to love as you loved. May your mercy and compassion overflow from our hearts to others.

JOURNALING

What can you value about someone you personally find hard to love?

_____

_____

_____

_____

_____

_____

_____

_____

_____

_____

_____

_____

_____

_____

_____

_____

_____

_____

FOR FURTHER READING

To complete the books of 1 and 2 Peter during this twelve-part study, read 1 Peter 3:8–22. For more Bible passages on loving people, read Matthew 5:43–48; John 13:34–35; Romans 12:9–10; 1 Corinthians 13:1–13; 1 Thessalonians 4:9–10; 1 John 3:16–18; 4:7–21; and 2 John 1:5–6.

JOYFUL SERVICE

*As each one has received a gift, minister
it to one another, as good stewards
of the manifold grace of God.*
1 Peter 4:10 NKJV

61

REFLECTION

The joy that emerges from serving others can often be unexpected. Think of a time when you found great joy in serving in your church or community. What made that experience joyful for you? When have you experienced joy in using your spiritual gift to serve someone else?

_____

_____

_____

_____

_____

_____

_____

_____

_____

_____

_____

SITUATION

Peter has been calling believers in Christ to persevere in their faith even in the midst of trials, struggles, and adversities. He continually points them to the example of Jesus, who chose to endure suffering for their sake and give up his mortal life so they could experience eternal life. In this portion of his letter, Peter calls believers to focus on this hope they have been given and look forward to the imminent return of Christ. He also calls them to band together as a community by loving one another, showing hospitality, and joyfully *serving* one another.

OBSERVATION

Read 1 Peter 4:1–11 from the New International
Version or the New King James Version.

NEW INTERNATIONAL VERSION

[1] Therefore, since Christ suffered in his body, arm yourselves also with the same attitude, because whoever suffers in the body is done with sin. [2] As a result, they do not live the rest of their earthly lives for evil human desires, but rather for the will of God. [3] For you have spent enough time in the past doing what pagans choose to do—living in debauchery, lust, drunkenness, orgies, carousing and detestable idolatry. [4] They are surprised that you do not join them in their reckless, wild living, and they heap abuse on you. [5] But they will have to give account to him who is ready to judge the living and the dead. [6] For this is the reason the gospel was preached even to those who are now dead, so that they might be judged according to human standards in regard to the body, but live according to God in regard to the spirit.

[7] The end of all things is near. Therefore be alert and of sober mind so that you may pray. [8] Above all, love each other deeply, because love covers over a multitude of sins. [9] Offer hospitality to one another without grumbling. [10] Each of you should use whatever gift you have received to serve others, as faithful stewards of God's grace in its various forms. [11] If anyone speaks, they should do so as one who speaks the very words of God. If anyone serves, they should do so with the strength God provides, so that in all things God may be praised through Jesus Christ. To him be the glory and the power for ever and ever. Amen.

NEW KING JAMES VERSION

[1] Therefore, since Christ suffered for us in the flesh, arm yourselves also with the same mind, for he who has suffered in the flesh has ceased from sin, [2] that he no longer should live the rest of his time in the flesh for the lusts of men, but for the will of God. [3] For we have spent enough of our

past lifetime in doing the will of the Gentiles—when we walked in lewdness, lusts, drunkenness, revelries, drinking parties, and abominable idolatries. ⁴ In regard to these, they think it strange that you do not run with them in the same flood of dissipation, speaking evil of you. ⁵ They will give an account to Him who is ready to judge the living and the dead. ⁶ For this reason the gospel was preached also to those who are dead, that they might be judged according to men in the flesh, but live according to God in the spirit.

⁷ But the end of all things is at hand; therefore be serious and watchful in your prayers. ⁸ And above all things have fervent love for one another, for "love will cover a multitude of sins." ⁹ Be hospitable to one another without grumbling. ¹⁰ As each one has received a gift, minister it to one another, as good stewards of the manifold grace of God. ¹¹ If anyone speaks, let him speak as the oracles of God. If anyone ministers, let him do it as with the ability which God supplies, that in all things God may be glorified through Jesus Christ, to whom belong the glory and the dominion forever and ever. Amen.

EXPLORATION

1. Peter writes that "whoever suffers in the body is done with sin" (verse 1). How have you seen trials make you a stronger believer in Christ and increase your faith?

_____

_____

_____

2. Peter's teaching is that *all* humans will face death and judgment, but those who are found righteous before God will be vindicated for their faithfulness. How does this give you hope?

_____

_____

_____

3. How do you respond to the statement that "love covers over a multitude of sins" (verse 8)? What do you think Peter is implying through these words?

4. What are some ways you can develop the gifts that God has given to you?

5. Think of someone who, in your opinion, used his or her gifts to serve God. How would you describe that person?

6. What is the purpose of the gifts and talents that God gives to his children?

INSPIRATION

"If anyone ministers, let him do it as with *the ability* which God supplies" (1 Peter 4:11 NKJV, emphasis added). Ability reveals destiny. What is your ability? What do you do well? What do people ask you to do again? What task comes easily? What topic keeps your attention? . . .

For twenty years I was the senior minister of our church. I was in the thick of it all: budgets, personnel issues, buildings, hiring, and firing. I was happy to fill the role. But I was happiest preaching and writing. My mind was always gravitating toward the next sermon, the next series. Even during committee meetings, *especially* during committee meetings, I was doodling on the next message.

As the church increased in number, so did the staff. More staff meant more people to manage. More people to manage meant spending more time doing what I didn't feel called to do. . . . I was blessed to have options. I was equally blessed to have a church that provided flexibility. I transitioned from senior minister to teaching minister.

When I became teaching minister, a few people were puzzled. "Don't you miss being the senior minister?" Translation: Weren't you demoted?

Earlier in my life I would have thought so. But I have come to see God's definition of promotion: a promotion is not a move up the ladder; it is a move toward your call. Don't let someone "promote" you out of your call. . . .

"Fan into flame the gift of God, which is *in you*" (2 Timothy 1:6, emphasis added). You be you. Don't be your parents or grandparents. You can admire them, appreciate them, and learn from them. But you cannot be them. You aren't them. . . .

Jesus was insistent on this. After the resurrection he appeared to some of his followers. He gave Peter a specific pastoral assignment that included great sacrifice. The apostle responded by pointing at John and saying, "Lord, what about him?" Jesus answered, "If I want him to remain alive until I return, what is that to you? You must follow me" (John 21:21–22).

In other words, don't occupy yourself with another person's assignment; stay focused on your own. (From *Glory Days* by Max Lucado.)

REACTION

7. What are some of the abilities God has given to you? What do you do well?

---

8. How are you using your abilities to be a faithful steward of God's grace?

---

9. How are you serving others in the "strength God provides" (verse 11)? How have you seen God use you to do things you didn't imagine were possible in your own strength?

---

10. How have you found joy in serving others?

---

11. What blessings have you received through serving others?

_____

_____

_____

_____

12. In what tangible way can you express your gratitude to God today for these talents and abilities that he has given to you?

_____

_____

_____

_____

LIFE LESSONS

Serving is easy when we are motivated and when we are using the gifts God has given us to do what he has called us to do. As believers in Christ, we are motivated to love and serve because we know that Jesus loved and came to serve us. Since he did so much for us, when none of us deserved it, how could we _not_ do all we can for him? Our best efforts at service represent the highest form of gratitude we can express to God for his gift of love and eternal life.

DEVOTION

Father, give us a deeper appreciation for what you have done for us and new enthusiasm for serving you. Show us how to extend your love to others. Help us to turn to you for wisdom, strength, and perseverance. We give you all the glory for what you will accomplish through us.

JOURNALING

How does reflecting on what Jesus has done for you motivate you to serve others?

FOR FURTHER READING

To complete the books of 1 and 2 Peter during this twelve-part study, read 1 Peter 4:1–11. For more Bible passages on serving, read Deuteronomy 10:12; Joshua 22:5; Matthew 20:26–28; Romans 12:11; 2 Corinthians 9:12; Galatians 5:13; Ephesians 6:6–8; and Colossians 3:23–24.

TRUSTING GOD THROUGH TRIALS

So then, those who suffer according to God's will should commit themselves to their faithful Creator and continue to do good.

1 PETER 4:19

REFLECTION

Talking about God's faithfulness as a general concept is quite different from experiencing it personally. Think of a time when God proved his trustworthiness to you. It may have been in a difficult situation or in a happy situation. How did that experience stretch your faith?

SITUATION

Peter had endured a number of trials for his belief in Christ. In the book of Acts, we read how he was arrested for sharing the message of Jesus in the Temple, brought before the high priest, and almost put to death by the ruling council (see 5:12–33). Later, he was arrested and imprisoned at the order of King Herod, though God orchestrated his escape (see 12:1–11). For Peter, it was not a mystery as to why believers would, at times, have to endure suffering for the sake of the gospel. However, that suffering should not come as a result of our wrong actions. Peter wanted us to know that the consequences for sin are real—and we need to obey God.

OBSERVATION

Read 1 Peter 4:12–19 from the New International
Version or the New King James Version.

NEW INTERNATIONAL VERSION

¹² Dear friends, do not be surprised at the fiery ordeal that has come on you to test you, as though something strange were happening to you. ¹³ But rejoice inasmuch as you participate in the sufferings of Christ, so that you may be overjoyed when his glory is revealed. ¹⁴ If you are insulted because of the name of Christ, you are blessed, for the Spirit of glory and of God rests on you. ¹⁵ If you suffer, it should not be as a murderer or thief or any other kind of criminal, or even as a meddler. ¹⁶ However, if you suffer as a Christian, do not be ashamed, but praise God that you bear that name. ¹⁷ For it is time for judgment to begin with God's household; and if it begins with us, what will the outcome be for those who do not obey the gospel of God? ¹⁸ And,

> "If it is hard for the righteous to be saved,
> what will become of the ungodly and the sinner?"

¹⁹ So then, those who suffer according to God's will should commit themselves to their faithful Creator and continue to do good.

NEW KING JAMES VERSION

¹² Beloved, do not think it strange concerning the fiery trial which is to try you, as though some strange thing happened to you; ¹³ but rejoice to the extent that you partake of Christ's sufferings, that when His glory is revealed, you may also be glad with exceeding joy. ¹⁴ If you are reproached for the name of Christ, blessed are you, for the Spirit of glory and of God rests upon you. On their part He is blasphemed, but on your part He is glorified. ¹⁵ But let none of you suffer as a murderer, a thief, an evildoer, or as a busybody in other people's matters. ¹⁶ Yet if anyone

suffers as a Christian, let him not be ashamed, but let him glorify God in this matter.

¹⁷ For the time has come for judgment to begin at the house of God; and if it begins with us first, what will be the end of those who do not obey the gospel of God? ¹⁸ Now

> "If the righteous one is scarcely saved,
> Where will the ungodly and the sinner appear?"

¹⁹ Therefore let those who suffer according to the will of God commit their souls to Him in doing good, as to a faithful Creator.

EXPLORATION

1. Why does Peter say you should not be surprised at the ordeals that come in life?

_____

_____

_____

_____

_____

2. What does it mean to "participate in the sufferings of Christ" (verse 13)?

_____

_____

_____

_____

3. Why should you rejoice if you are insulted because you are following Christ?

4. How does Peter distinguish between the suffering caused by one's own actions and the suffering that comes from faithfully pursuing Christ?

5. Peter says that "it is time for judgment to begin with God's household" (verse 17). What does Peter mean by this in the context of believers facing persecution for their faith?

6. In what way can suffering actually be a blessing to you?

INSPIRATION

Is there anything more frail than a bruised reed? Look at the bruised reed at the water's edge. A once slender and tall stalk of sturdy river grass, it is now bowed and bent.

Are you a bruised reed? Was it so long ago that you stood so tall, so proud? You were upright and sturdy, nourished by the waters and rooted in the riverbed of confidence.

Then something happened. You were bruised . . . by harsh words

by a friend's anger

by a spouse's betrayal by your own failure by religion's rigidity.

And you were wounded, bent ever so slightly. Your hollow reed, once erect, now stooped, and hidden in the bulrush.

And the smoldering wick on the candle. Is there anything closer to death than a smoldering wick? Once aflame, now flickering and failing. Still warm from yesterday's passion, but no fire. Not yet cold, but far from hot. Was it that long ago you blazed with faith? Remember how you illuminated the path?

Then came the wind . . . the cold wind, the harsh wind. They said your ideas were foolish. They told you your dreams were too lofty. They scolded you for challenging the time-tested. The constant wind wore down upon you. Oh, you stood strong for a moment (or maybe a lifetime), but the endless blast whipped your flickering flame, leaving you one pinch away from darkness.

The bruised reed and the smoldering wick. Society knows what to do with you. The world has a place for the beaten. The world will break you off; the world will snuff you out.

But the artists of Scripture proclaim that God won't. Painted on canvas after canvas is the tender touch of a Creator who has a special place for the bruised and weary of the world. A God who is the friend of the wounded heart. A God who is the keeper of your dreams. (From *He Still Moves Stones* by Max Lucado.)

REACTION

7. When are some times you felt like the bruised reed or the smoldering wick?

_____

_____

_____

_____

_____

8. What hope is there for those who are emotionally wounded?

_____

_____

_____

9. What can you do to develop a faith that will withstand pressure and persecution?

_____

_____

_____

_____

10. In what ways have you suffered because of your faith in Jesus Christ?

_____

_____

_____

_____

11. How has God used that pain and suffering in your life for good?

_____

_____

_____

_____

12. In practical terms, how can you trust God to help you through difficult times in your life?

_____

_____

_____

_____

LIFE LESSONS

Life has a way of riding roughshod over our expectations and leaving us feeling disappointed. Peter doesn't tell us to avoid expectations—he simply gives us some guidelines about what to expect. One wise expectation involves the fact that God can use any circumstance to bring about good for us . . . even when the hardship is clearly as a result of something that we have done. That's why we must always trust our souls to our faithful Creator. He is trustworthy.

DEVOTION

Father, you never said this life would be easy. Instead, you warned us to expect pain and troubles. But you also promised that you would be with us. Father, teach us to rely on you so that we can withstand the struggles and storms that come our way. And even when we cannot understand why you are allowing us to suffer, help us to trust you.

JOURNALING

How will you thank God today for the trials in your life?

FOR FURTHER READING

To complete the books of 1 and 2 Peter during this twelve-part study, read 1 Peter 4:12–19. For more Bible passages on persevering through trials, read Romans 8:17–18; 2 Corinthians 1:5–7; Philippians 1:29; 3:10; 1 Thessalonians 3:3–4; 2 Thessalonians 1:3–4; 2 Timothy 1:8; Hebrews 12:10–11; and James 1:2–4.

GRACE TO THE HUMBLE

Therefore humble yourselves under the mighty hand of God, that He may exalt you in due time, casting all your care upon Him, for He cares for you.
1 Peter 5:6–7 NKJV

REFLECTION

Humility is an elusive personal quality. It suddenly vanishes just when you realize you've got it! It generally takes the observations of others to confirm any progress in humility. What are some things others have said about you in this regard? What would you *like* them to say about you?

SITUATION

Peter, having outlined some of the fundamentals of the Christian faith and providing his readers with reasons to persevere during trials, concludes with a word aimed at the younger and older members in the church. Peter first encourages the elders to be faithful "shepherds" of the congregation and then urges the younger members to submit to them and show their respect. In this, Peter is likely thinking about the present and future leadership of the church, for he knows believers have an adversary that roams about "like a roaring lion" (5:8), seeking to destroy them. Peter calls on the believers to not let the enemy come between them but to instead humble themselves before God so he can give them grace and lift them up in due time.

OBSERVATION

Read 1 Peter 5:1–14 from the New International
Version or the New King James Version.

NEW INTERNATIONAL VERSION

[1] To the elders among you, I appeal as a fellow elder and a witness of Christ's sufferings who also will share in the glory to be revealed: [2] Be shepherds of God's flock that is under your care, watching over them—not because you must, but because you are willing, as God wants you to be; not pursuing dishonest gain, but eager to serve; [3] not lording it over those entrusted to you, but being examples to the flock. [4] And when the Chief Shepherd appears, you will receive the crown of glory that will never fade away.

[5] In the same way, you who are younger, submit yourselves to your elders. All of you, clothe yourselves with humility toward one another, because,

> "God opposes the proud
>   but shows favor to the humble."

[6] Humble yourselves, therefore, under God's mighty hand, that he may lift you up in due time. [7] Cast all your anxiety on him because he cares for you.

[8] Be alert and of sober mind. Your enemy the devil prowls around like a roaring lion looking for someone to devour. [9] Resist him, standing firm in the faith, because you know that the family of believers throughout the world is undergoing the same kind of sufferings.

[10] And the God of all grace, who called you to his eternal glory in Christ, after you have suffered a little while, will himself restore you and make you strong, firm and steadfast. [11] To him be the power for ever and ever. Amen.

[12] With the help of Silas, whom I regard as a faithful brother, I have written to you briefly, encouraging you and testifying that this is the true grace of God. Stand fast in it.

[13] She who is in Babylon, chosen together with you, sends you her greetings, and so does my son Mark. [14] Greet one another with a kiss of love.

Peace to all of you who are in Christ.

NEW KING JAMES VERSION

[1] The elders who are among you I exhort, I who am a fellow elder and a witness of the sufferings of Christ, and also a partaker of the glory that will be revealed: [2] Shepherd the flock of God which is among you, serving as overseers, not by compulsion but willingly, not for dishonest gain but eagerly; [3] nor as being lords over those entrusted to you, but being examples to the flock; [4] and when the Chief Shepherd appears, you will receive the crown of glory that does not fade away.

[5] Likewise you younger people, submit yourselves to your elders. Yes, all of you be submissive to one another, and be clothed with humility, for

> "God resists the proud,
> But gives grace to the humble."

[6] Therefore humble yourselves under the mighty hand of God, that He may exalt you in due time, [7] casting all your care upon Him, for He cares for you.

[8] Be sober, be vigilant; because your adversary the devil walks about like a roaring lion, seeking whom he may devour. [9] Resist him, steadfast in the faith, knowing that the same sufferings are experienced by your brotherhood in the world. [10] But may the God of all grace, who called us to His eternal glory by Christ Jesus, after you have suffered a while, perfect, establish, strengthen, and settle you. [11] To Him be the glory and the dominion forever and ever. Amen.

[12] By Silvanus, our faithful brother as I consider him, I have written to you briefly, exhorting and testifying that this is the true grace of God in which you stand.

¹³ She who is in Babylon, elect together with you, greets you; and so does Mark my son. ¹⁴ Greet one another with a kiss of love.

Peace to you all who are in Christ Jesus. Amen.

EXPLORATION

1. What are some of the responsibilities that Peter lists of church leaders?

_____

_____

_____

2. How have you exercised or experienced these responsibilities?

_____

_____

_____

3. In what way does a spirit of humility among believers benefit the church?

_____

_____

_____

4. How does God reward those who are humble before him?

_____

_____

_____

5. What are some of the ways God helps believers to remain faithful to him?

_____

_____

_____

6. What kind of future can God's people anticipate?

_____

_____

_____

INSPIRATION

When he wasn't flying his private jet across the Atlantic or watching sunsets from the deck of one of his yachts, he was living a life of luxury inside his ten-thousand-square-foot Lexington Avenue penthouse in New York City.

His yacht *Bull* cost seven million dollars. His jet cost twenty-four million. He had a home in France, a beach home in Montauk, and a house in Palm Beach. He had boats and cars. His wife had furs and designer handbags, Wedgewood china, and Christofle silver. . . .

Everyone wanted to know him. People stood in line to shake his hand. People like Steven Spielberg and Elie Wiesel. To stand in his Manhattan office was to stand in the epicenter of investment success.

Or so it seemed until the morning of December 10, 2008. That's when the charade ended. That's when Bernie Madoff, this generation's most infamous scam artist, sat down with his wife and two sons and confessed that it was a giant Ponzi scheme . . . just one big lie.

Over the next days, weeks, and months, the staggering details became public knowledge. Madoff had masterminded a twenty-year-long shell game, the largest financial crime in US history. He had swindled people out of billions of dollars.

His collapse was of biblical proportions. In short order he was stripped of everything. No money. No future. No family. One of his sons committed suicide. His wife went into seclusion. And seventy-one-year-old Bernie Madoff was sentenced to spend the rest of his life as prisoner number 61727-054 in the Federal Correction Complex of Butner, North Carolina.

Why did he do it? What makes a man live a lie for decades? . . .

Stature. Madoff was addicted to adulation. He was hooked on recognition. He wanted the applause of people, and money was his way of earning it. He elbowed and clawed his way to the top of the mountain, only to discover that its peak is slippery and crowded. If only he had known this promise: "God resists the proud, but gives grace to the humble" (1 Peter 5:5 NKJV).

Why the strong language? Why the blanket condemnation? How do we explain God's abhorrence of the haughty heart?

Simple. God resists the proud because the proud resist God. Arrogance stiffens the knee so it will not kneel, hardens the heart so it will not admit to sin. The heart of pride never confesses, never repents, never asks for forgiveness. Indeed, the arrogant never feel the need for forgiveness. Pride is the hidden reef that shipwrecks the soul. (From *Unshakable Hope* by Max Lucado.)

REACTION

7. Why is pride so dangerous? Why does God oppose it so strongly in Scripture?

_____

_____

_____

_____

_____

8. Why is it difficult to be humble? How can you protect yourself from the sin of pride?

_____

_____

_____

_____

9. What are some of the signs or evidences of pride?

_____

_____

_____

10. What does Peter say is the antidote to pride?

_____

_____

_____

11. What promise are you given if you choose to humble yourself before God?

_____

_____

_____

12. What does it mean to be "alert and of sober mind"? How can this help you to resist the attacks of the devil, who "prowls around like a roaring lion" (verse 8)?

_____

_____

_____

LIFE LESSONS

A starting point in practicing humility comes when we realize there's no such thing as a humble feeling. There are humble _actions_, and most of them go unnoticed by anyone else. If we demand to be noticed, we're not acting in humility. This is why Jesus' example has such power for us. When we are imitating him, we are carrying out humble actions. These will almost always involve loving others and doing acts of service for others.

DEVOTION

Father, thank you for sending your Son to show us how to become servant leaders. Give us the grace to follow his example. Open our eyes to the blind spots in our lives and help us root out any trace of pride. Thank you for your promise that, at the right time, you will lift up the humble.

JOURNALING

In what areas of your life do you feel you need more humility?

FOR FURTHER READING

To complete the books of 1 and 2 Peter during this twelve-part study, read 1 Peter 5:1–14. For more Bible passages on humility, read Proverbs 11:2; 15:33; Zephaniah 2:3; Luke 14:11; Ephesians 4:2; Philippians 2:3; Colossians 3:12; and James 4:10.

LESSON TEN

SELF-DISCIPLINE

*Make every effort to add to your faith
goodness; and to goodness, knowledge; and
to knowledge, self-control; and to self-control,
perseverance; and to perseverance, godliness.*

2 PETER 1:5–6

REFLECTION

"Spiritual disciplines" such as prayer, Bible reading, worship, and fasting have long been practiced as a means to sharpen spiritual awareness, correct bad habits, and grow spiritually. What spiritual disciplines have helped you the most in your journey with Christ? Why?

_____

_____

_____

_____

_____

_____

_____

_____

_____

_____

SITUATION

By the time Peter penned his second letter, he was aware his life on earth would soon be coming to an end. However, rather than wallow in self-pity, he chooses to begin his final letter with a tribute to his Lord and Savior. He wants to show his readers that as long as they focus their faith on Jesus, they have everything they need to meet any challenge—and even confront death itself. He reminds them of how God is working in their lives and the promises they have received in Christ. Peter's desire for them—and us—is to keep on growing and add to their lives the "fruit" of goodness, knowledge, self-control, perseverance, godliness, affection, and love.

OBSERVATION

Read 2 Peter 1:1–21 from the New International Version or the New King James Version.

NEW INTERNATIONAL VERSION

[1] Simon Peter, a servant and apostle of Jesus Christ,

To those who through the righteousness of our God and Savior Jesus Christ have received a faith as precious as ours:

[2] Grace and peace be yours in abundance through the knowledge of God and of Jesus our Lord.

[3] His divine power has given us everything we need for a godly life through our knowledge of him who called us by his own glory and goodness. [4] Through these he has given us his very great and precious promises, so that through them you may participate in the divine nature, having escaped the corruption in the world caused by evil desires.

[5] For this very reason, make every effort to add to your faith goodness; and to goodness, knowledge; [6] and to knowledge, self-control; and to self-control, perseverance; and to perseverance, godliness; [7] and to godliness, mutual affection; and to mutual affection, love. [8] For if you possess these qualities in increasing measure, they will keep you from being ineffective and unproductive in your knowledge of our Lord Jesus Christ. [9] But whoever does not have them is nearsighted and blind, forgetting that they have been cleansed from their past sins.

[10] Therefore, my brothers and sisters, make every effort to confirm your calling and election. For if you do these things, you will never stumble, [11] and you will receive a rich welcome into the eternal kingdom of our Lord and Savior Jesus Christ.

[12] So I will always remind you of these things, even though you know them and are firmly established in the truth you now have. [13] I think it is right to refresh your memory as long as I live in the tent of this body, [14] because I know that I will soon put it aside, as our Lord Jesus Christ

has made clear to me. ¹⁵ And I will make every effort to see that after my departure you will always be able to remember these things.

¹⁶ For we did not follow cleverly devised stories when we told you about the coming of our Lord Jesus Christ in power, but we were eyewitnesses of his majesty. ¹⁷ He received honor and glory from God the Father when the voice came to him from the Majestic Glory, saying, "This is my Son, whom I love; with him I am well pleased." ¹⁸ We ourselves heard this voice that came from heaven when we were with him on the sacred mountain.

¹⁹ We also have the prophetic message as something completely reliable, and you will do well to pay attention to it, as to a light shining in a dark place, until the day dawns and the morning star rises in your hearts. ²⁰ Above all, you must understand that no prophecy of Scripture came about by the prophet's own interpretation of things. ²¹ For prophecy never had its origin in the human will, but prophets, though human, spoke from God as they were carried along by the Holy Spirit.

New King James Version

¹ Simon Peter, a bondservant and apostle of Jesus Christ,

To those who have obtained like precious faith with us by the righteousness of our God and Savior Jesus Christ:

² Grace and peace be multiplied to you in the knowledge of God and of Jesus our Lord, ³ as His divine power has given to us all things that pertain to life and godliness, through the knowledge of Him who called us by glory and virtue, ⁴ by which have been given to us exceedingly great and precious promises, that through these you may be partakers of the divine nature, having escaped the corruption that is in the world through lust.

⁵ But also for this very reason, giving all diligence, add to your faith virtue, to virtue knowledge, ⁶ to knowledge self-control, to self-control perseverance, to perseverance godliness, ⁷ to godliness brotherly kindness, and to brotherly kindness love. ⁸ For if these things are yours and abound, you will be neither barren nor unfruitful in the knowledge of our

Lord Jesus Christ. [9] For he who lacks these things is shortsighted, even to blindness, and has forgotten that he was cleansed from his old sins.

[10] Therefore, brethren, be even more diligent to make your call and election sure, for if you do these things you will never stumble; [11] for so an entrance will be supplied to you abundantly into the everlasting kingdom of our Lord and Savior Jesus Christ.

[12] For this reason I will not be negligent to remind you always of these things, though you know and are established in the present truth. [13] Yes, I think it is right, as long as I am in this tent, to stir you up by reminding you, [14] knowing that shortly I must put off my tent, just as our Lord Jesus Christ showed me. [15] Moreover I will be careful to ensure that you always have a reminder of these things after my decease.

[16] For we did not follow cunningly devised fables when we made known to you the power and coming of our Lord Jesus Christ, but were eyewitnesses of His majesty. [17] For He received from God the Father honor and glory when such a voice came to Him from the Excellent Glory: "This is My beloved Son, in whom I am well pleased." [18] And we heard this voice which came from heaven when we were with Him on the holy mountain.

[19] And so we have the prophetic word confirmed, which you do well to heed as a light that shines in a dark place, until the day dawns and the morning star rises in your hearts; [20] knowing this first, that no prophecy of Scripture is of any private interpretation, [21] for prophecy never came by the will of man, but holy men of God spoke as they were moved by the Holy Spirit.

EXPLORATION

1. What does it mean to "participate in the divine nature" of God (verse 4)?

----

2. What are some of the character traits that Peter says you need to possess?

3. What is the process for developing these character traits?

4. What does Peter say will happen if you possess these qualities in increasing measure?

5. What does it mean to "confirm your calling and election" (verse 10)?

6. How can you trust what you read and study in the Bible?

INSPIRATION

Though he creates, God was never created. Though he makes, he was never made. Though he causes, he was never caused. Hence the psalmist's proclamation: "Before the mountains were born or you brought forth the earth and the world, from everlasting to everlasting you are God" (Psalm 90:2).

God is Yahweh—an unchanging God, an uncaused God, and an ungoverned God.

You and I are governed. The weather determines what we wear. The terrain tells us how to travel. Gravity dictates our speed, and health determines our strength. We may challenge these forces and alter them slightly, but we never remove them.

God—our Shepherd—doesn't check the weather; he makes it. He doesn't defy gravity; he created it. He isn't affected by health; he has no body. Jesus said, "God is spirit" (John 4:24). Since he has no body; he has no limitation—equally active in Cambodia as he is in Connecticut. "Where can I go from your Spirit?" asked David. "Where can I flee from your presence? If I go up to the heavens, you are there; if I make my bed in the depths, you are there" (Psalm 139:7–8).

Unchanging. Uncaused. Ungoverned. These are only a fraction of God's qualities, but aren't they enough to give you a glimpse of your Father? Don't we need this kind of shepherd? Don't we need an unchanging shepherd?

When Lloyd Douglas, author of *The Robe* and other novels, attended college, he lived in a boardinghouse. A retired, wheelchair-bound music professor resided on the first floor. Each morning Douglas would stick his head in the door of the teacher's apartment and ask the same question, "Well, what's the good news?" The old man would pick up his tuning fork, tap it on the side of the wheel chair, and say, "That's middle C! It was middle C yesterday; it will be middle C tomorrow; it will be middle C a thousand years from now. The tenor upstairs sings flat. The piano across the hall is out of tune, but, my friend, that is middle C."

You and I need a middle *C*. Haven't you had enough change in your life? Relationships change. Health changes. The weather changes. But the Yahweh who ruled the earth last night is the same Yahweh who rules it today. Same convictions. Same plan. Same mood. Same love. He never changes. You can no more alter God than a pebble can alter the rhythm of the Pacific. Yahweh is our middle *C*. A still point in a turning world. Don't we need a still point? Don't we need an unchanging shepherd? (From *Traveling Light* by Max Lucado.)

REACTION

7. How does this description of your unchanging God challenge you to keep growing in him? What does it mean to "add to your faith" (verse 5)?

_____

_____

_____

_____

8. Why is self-discipline (self-control) so important?

_____

_____

_____

9. What results from spiritual discipline?

_____

_____

_____

10. How can a lack of discipline hinder your spiritual growth?

_____

_____

11. What is the difference between being disciplined and being legalistic?

_____

_____

_____

_____

12. What practical steps can you take to become more productive as a Christian?

_____

_____

_____

_____

LIFE LESSONS

Spiritual disciplines are chosen pathways of spiritual growth. They are spiritual actions we take to train our soul. They are decisions we make to develop our spiritual sensitivity to God in certain areas. Since God is unchanging, "closeness" to him requires movement and change on _our_ part, not his. In Jesus Christ, God has come toward us as far as he can. What are we doing to move in his direction? How are we deliberately becoming like Jesus? In what way will we imitate Christ today? Our answer will require some aspect of spiritual discipline.

DEVOTION

Father, you know our weaknesses. We need you to come alongside us and help us. We ask you to guide us and give us discipline so we can grow in our knowledge of you. Show us how much more you want to teach us. May we always hear your voice and obey.

JOURNALING

What spiritual discipline do you need to add to your life? How will you start?

_____

_____

_____

_____

_____

_____

_____

_____

_____

_____

_____

_____

_____

_____

_____

_____

_____

FOR FURTHER READING

To complete the books of 1 and 2 Peter during this twelve-part study, read 2 Peter 1:1–21. For more Bible passages on self-discipline, read Proverbs 1:1–7; Matthew 5:27–30; 1 Corinthians 10:12–13; 1 Thessalonians 5:6–8; 2 Timothy 1:7; Titus 1:7–8; 2:2–8; and James 1:19–21.

FALSE TEACHERS

*But there were also false prophets among the
people, even as there will be false teachers
among you, who will secretly bring in destructive
heresies, even denying the Lord who bought them,
and bring on themselves swift destruction.*
2 PETER 2:1 NKJV

REFLECTION

We are often impressed more with a teacher's style and charisma than with the veracity of his or her words. How do we avoid being taken in by an untruthful teacher? How can we avoid missing the benefits of a true instructor? Think of a time when you were impressed by a dynamic preacher. What do you remember most about the preacher's message?

SITUATION

Peter's desire is for his readers to hold on to the truths they have received about their salvation so that after his "departure" from this world, they will not be persuaded by false teaching. He has reminded the believers of his own eyewitness accounts of Jesus' life and how the Old Testament prophets pointed to Christ as the Messiah. But just as there were also false prophets in the days of old, so there will be false teachers in our day and age. Yet, as Peter notes, we can recognize them as such by their character—and be assured they will be condemned.

OBSERVATION

Read 2 Peter 2:1–22 from the New International
Version or the New King James Version.

NEW INTERNATIONAL VERSION

[1] But there were also false prophets among the people, just as there will be false teachers among you. They will secretly introduce destructive heresies, even denying the sovereign Lord who bought them—bringing swift destruction on themselves. [2] Many will follow their depraved conduct and will bring the way of truth into disrepute. [3] In their greed these teachers will exploit you with fabricated stories. Their condemnation has long been hanging over them, and their destruction has not been sleeping.

[4] For if God did not spare angels when they sinned, but sent them to hell, putting them in chains of darkness to be held for judgment; [5] if he did not spare the ancient world when he brought the flood on its ungodly people, but protected Noah, a preacher of righteousness, and seven others; [6] if he condemned the cities of Sodom and Gomorrah by burning them to ashes, and made them an example of what is going to happen to the ungodly; [7] and if he rescued Lot, a righteous man, who was distressed by the depraved conduct of the lawless [8] (for that righteous man, living among them day after day, was tormented in his righteous soul by the lawless deeds he saw and heard)— [9] if this is so, then the Lord knows how to rescue the godly from trials and to hold the unrighteous for punishment on the day of judgment. [10] This is especially true of those who follow the corrupt desire of the flesh and despise authority.

Bold and arrogant, they are not afraid to heap abuse on celestial beings; [11] yet even angels, although they are stronger and more powerful, do not heap abuse on such beings when bringing judgment on them from the Lord. [12] But these people blaspheme in matters they do not understand. They are like unreasoning animals, creatures of instinct, born only to be caught and destroyed, and like animals they too will perish.

¹³ They will be paid back with harm for the harm they have done. Their idea of pleasure is to carouse in broad daylight. They are blots and blemishes, reveling in their pleasures while they feast with you. ¹⁴ With eyes full of adultery, they never stop sinning; they seduce the unstable; they are experts in greed—an accursed brood! ¹⁵ They have left the straight way and wandered off to follow the way of Balaam son of Bezer, who loved the wages of wickedness. ¹⁶ But he was rebuked for his wrongdoing by a donkey—an animal without speech—who spoke with a human voice and restrained the prophet's madness.

¹⁷ These people are springs without water and mists driven by a storm. Blackest darkness is reserved for them. ¹⁸ For they mouth empty, boastful words and, by appealing to the lustful desires of the flesh, they entice people who are just escaping from those who live in error. ¹⁹ They promise them freedom, while they themselves are slaves of depravity—for "people are slaves to whatever has mastered them." ²⁰ If they have escaped the corruption of the world by knowing our Lord and Savior Jesus Christ and are again entangled in it and are overcome, they are worse off at the end than they were at the beginning. ²¹ It would have been better for them not to have known the way of righteousness, than to have known it and then to turn their backs on the sacred command that was passed on to them. ²² Of them the proverbs are true: "A dog returns to its vomit," and, "A sow that is washed returns to her wallowing in the mud."

New King James Version

¹ But there were also false prophets among the people, even as there will be false teachers among you, who will secretly bring in destructive heresies, even denying the Lord who bought them, and bring on themselves swift destruction. ² And many will follow their destructive ways, because of whom the way of truth will be blasphemed. ³ By covetousness they will exploit you with deceptive words; for a long time their judgment has not been idle, and their destruction does not slumber.

⁴ For if God did not spare the angels who sinned, but cast them down to hell and delivered them into chains of darkness, to be reserved for

judgment; [5] and did not spare the ancient world, but saved Noah, one of eight people, a preacher of righteousness, bringing in the flood on the world of the ungodly; [6] and turning the cities of Sodom and Gomorrah into ashes, condemned them to destruction, making them an example to those who afterward would live ungodly; [7] and delivered righteous Lot, who was oppressed by the filthy conduct of the wicked [8] (for that righteous man, dwelling among them, tormented his righteous soul from day to day by seeing and hearing their lawless deeds)— [9] then the Lord knows how to deliver the godly out of temptations and to reserve the unjust under punishment for the day of judgment, [10] and especially those who walk according to the flesh in the lust of uncleanness and despise authority. They are presumptuous, self-willed. They are not afraid to speak evil of dignitaries, [11] whereas angels, who are greater in power and might, do not bring a reviling accusation against them before the Lord.

[12] But these, like natural brute beasts made to be caught and destroyed, speak evil of the things they do not understand, and will utterly perish in their own corruption, [13] and will receive the wages of unrighteousness, as those who count it pleasure to carouse in the daytime. They are spots and blemishes, carousing in their own deceptions while they feast with you, [14] having eyes full of adultery and that cannot cease from sin, enticing unstable souls. They have a heart trained in covetous practices, and are accursed children. [15] They have forsaken the right way and gone astray, following the way of Balaam the son of Beor, who loved the wages of unrighteousness; [16] but he was rebuked for his iniquity: a dumb donkey speaking with a man's voice restrained the madness of the prophet.

[17] These are wells without water, clouds carried by a tempest, for whom is reserved the blackness of darkness forever.

[18] For when they speak great swelling words of emptiness, they allure through the lusts of the flesh, through lewdness, the ones who have actually escaped from those who live in error. [19] While they promise them liberty, they themselves are slaves of corruption; for by whom a person is overcome, by him also he is brought into bondage. [20] For if, after they have escaped the pollutions of the world through the knowledge of the

Lord and Savior Jesus Christ, they are again entangled in them and overcome, the latter end is worse for them than the beginning. [21] For it would have been better for them not to have known the way of righteousness, than having known it, to turn from the holy commandment delivered to them. [22] But it has happened to them according to the true proverb: "A dog returns to his own vomit," and, "a sow, having washed, to her wallowing in the mire."

EXPLORATION

1. What does Peter say false teachers do? Why do people follow them?

_____

_____

_____

_____

_____

_____

2. What motivates false teachers to work their way into churches?

_____

_____

_____

_____

_____

_____

3. What are some of the historical events Peter lists that show God's justice?

_____

_____

_____

_____

4. What kind of tactics do false teachers use to gain followers?

_____

_____

_____

5. Why will there be certain punishment for those who turn others away from God?

_____

_____

_____

6. How can you recognize false teachers for what they truly are?

_____

_____

_____

INSPIRATION

Voices. They whisper. They woo. They taunt. They tantalize. They flirt. They flatter. "Go ahead, it's okay." "Just wait until tomorrow." "Don't worry, no one will know." "How could anything that feels so right be so wrong?"

The voices of the crowd.

Our lives are Wall Streets of chaos, stock markets loud with demands. Grown men and women barking in a frenzied effort to get all they can before time runs out. "Buy. Sell. Trade. Swap. But whatever you do, do it fast—and loud." A carnival of gray-flannel suits where no one smiles and everyone dashes. An endless chorus of booming voices: some offering, some taking, and all screaming.

What do we do with the voices?

As I write this, I'm seated at a desk in a hotel room. I'm away from home. Away from people who know me. Away from family members who love me.

Voices that encourage and affirm are distant. But voices that tantalize and entice are near. Although the room is quiet, if I listen, their voices are crystal clear.

A placard on my nightstand invites me to a lounge in the lobby, where I can "make new friends in a relaxing atmosphere." An advertisement on top of the television promises me that with the request of a late-night adult movie my "fantasies will come true." In the phone book, several columns of escort services offer "love away from home." . . .

Voices. Some for pleasure. Some for power. Some promise acceptance. Some promise tenderness. But all promise something. Even the voices that Jesus heard promised something.

"After the people saw the miraculous sign that Jesus did, they began to say, 'Surely this is the Prophet who is to come into the world'" (John 6:14).

To the casual observer, these are the voices of victory. To the untrained ear, these are the sounds of triumph. What could be better? Five thousand men plus women and children proclaiming Christ to be the prophet. Thousands of voices swelling into a roar of revival, an ovation of adulation . . .

Jesus heard the voices. He heard the lurings. But he also heard someone else. And when Jesus heard him, he sought him. "Jesus, knowing that they intended to come and make him king by force, withdrew again to a mountain by himself" (John 6:15).

Jesus preferred to be alone with the true God rather than in a crowd with the wrong people. Logic didn't tell him to dismiss the crowds. Conventional wisdom didn't tell him to turn his back on a willing army. No, it wasn't a voice from without that Jesus heard. It was a voice from within.

The mark of a sheep is its ability to hear the Shepherd's voice. "The sheep listen to his voice. He calls his own sheep by name and leads them out" (John 10:3). The mark of a disciple is his or her ability to hear the Master's voice. (From *In the Eye of the Storm* by Max Lucado.)

REACTION

7. What are some of the affirming voices in your world? What are some of the negative that compete for your time and attention?

_____

_____

_____

_____

_____

8. How did Jesus resist the voices that made false promises to him?

_____

_____

_____

_____

9. There are times when you will need to confront and expose sin in the lives of other believers. What are some guidelines for deciding when this action is appropriate?

_____

_____

_____

_____

10. Why do believers sometimes downplay God's justice and judgment?

_____

_____

_____

_____

11. How is it helpful to know that God has judged evil throughout history?

_____

_____

_____

_____

12. How can you guard against the influence of the sin in the lives of people around you?

_____

_____

_____

LIFE LESSONS

Counterfeit money spotters spend a lot more time with the genuine articles than they spend with false versions. They are so familiar with the true bills they almost instinctively sense something wrong with a counterfeit even before they identify the evidence of fraud. Our best defense against false teachers involves spending time with Jesus. The better we know him, the more likely we will spot someone bending or twisting his words. The more we listen to his voice, the quicker we will react to the falseness in someone else's voice . . . no matter how charming the individual may be.

DEVOTION

Heavenly Father, you are a just and fair God. Please keep us safe from the influence of evil people. Help us to saturate ourselves with the truth of your Word so that we will easily recognize and expose false teaching. Father, reveal to us your truth so we may walk in it.

JOURNALING

What practical steps can you take to become a more discerning hearer of the truth?

FOR FURTHER READING

To complete the books of 1 and 2 Peter during this twelve-part study, read 2 Peter 2:1–22. For more Bible passages on the dangers of false teachers, read Isaiah 56:10–12; Jeremiah 23:2–4; Ezekiel 34:2–10; Matthew 7:15–23; John 10:12–13; Philippians 1:15–17; and 1 Timothy 6:3–5.

GOD IS IN CONTROL

*The Lord is not slow in keeping his promise,
as some understand slowness. Instead he is
patient with you, not wanting anyone to perish,
but everyone to come to repentance.*

2 PETER 3:9

REFLECTION

Our prayer life represents a constant growing edge in our relationship with God. Prayers that ask get answered, though we don't get to determine *how* God will answer. Think of a time when you were disappointed in how God answered one of your prayers. What did it take for you to realize that God's answer was best for you?

SITUATION

Peter closes his second letter much the same way as he began it—by confirming the hope of Jesus' return that all believers have and by reminding us that our trials for the sake of Christ *matter* to God. False teachers will scoff at this and claim Jesus will never return, but for them it will be like those who denied the flood was coming in the days of Noah and the Ark. Peter concludes with an endorsement of Paul's writings, affirming them as part of Scripture, and urges believers to remember the words of the prophets and the commands of Christ. Most of all, he desires us to remember that God is calling us to repentance . . . and is always in control.

OBSERVATION

*Read 2 Peter 3:1–18 from the New International
Version or the New King James Version.*

New International Version

¹ Dear friends, this is now my second letter to you. I have written both of them as reminders to stimulate you to wholesome thinking. ² I want you to recall the words spoken in the past by the holy prophets and the command given by our Lord and Savior through your apostles.

³ Above all, you must understand that in the last days scoffers will come, scoffing and following their own evil desires. ⁴ They will say, "Where is this 'coming' he promised? Ever since our ancestors died, everything goes on as it has since the beginning of creation." ⁵ But they deliberately forget that long ago by God's word the heavens came into being and the earth was formed out of water and by water. ⁶ By these waters also the world of that time was deluged and destroyed. ⁷ By the same word the present heavens and earth are reserved for fire, being kept for the day of judgment and destruction of the ungodly.

⁸ But do not forget this one thing, dear friends: With the Lord a day is like a thousand years, and a thousand years are like a day. ⁹ The Lord is not slow in keeping his promise, as some understand slowness. Instead he is patient with you, not wanting anyone to perish, but everyone to come to repentance.

¹⁰ But the day of the Lord will come like a thief. The heavens will disappear with a roar; the elements will be destroyed by fire, and the earth and everything done in it will be laid bare.

¹¹ Since everything will be destroyed in this way, what kind of people ought you to be? You ought to live holy and godly lives ¹² as you look forward to the day of God and speed its coming. That day will bring about the destruction of the heavens by fire, and the elements will melt in the heat. ¹³ But in keeping with his promise we are looking forward to a new heaven and a new earth, where righteousness dwells.

¹⁴ So then, dear friends, since you are looking forward to this, make every effort to be found spotless, blameless and at peace with him. ¹⁵ Bear in mind that our Lord's patience means salvation, just as our dear brother Paul also wrote you with the wisdom that God gave him. ¹⁶ He writes the same way in all his letters, speaking in them of these matters. His letters contain some things that are hard to understand, which ignorant and unstable people distort, as they do the other Scriptures, to their own destruction.

¹⁷ Therefore, dear friends, since you have been forewarned, be on your guard so that you may not be carried away by the error of the lawless and fall from your secure position. ¹⁸ But grow in the grace and knowledge of our Lord and Savior Jesus Christ. To him be glory both now and forever! Amen.

New King James Version

¹ Beloved, I now write to you this second epistle (in both of which I stir up your pure minds by way of reminder), ² that you may be mindful of the words which were spoken before by the holy prophets, and of the commandment of us, the apostles of the Lord and Savior, ³ knowing this first: that scoffers will come in the last days, walking according to their own lusts, ⁴ and saying, "Where is the promise of His coming? For since the fathers fell asleep, all things continue as they were from the beginning of creation." ⁵ For this they willfully forget: that by the word of God the heavens were of old, and the earth standing out of water and in the water, ⁶ by which the world that then existed perished, being flooded with water. ⁷ But the heavens and the earth which are now preserved by the same word, are reserved for fire until the day of judgment and perdition of ungodly men.

⁸ But, beloved, do not forget this one thing, that with the Lord one day is as a thousand years, and a thousand years as one day. ⁹ The Lord is not slack concerning His promise, as some count slackness, but is longsuffering toward us, not willing that any should perish but that all should come to repentance.

¹⁰ But the day of the Lord will come as a thief in the night, in which the heavens will pass away with a great noise, and the elements will melt with fervent heat; both the earth and the works that are in it will be burned up. ¹¹ Therefore, since all these things will be dissolved, what manner of persons ought you to be in holy conduct and godliness, ¹² looking for and hastening the coming of the day of God, because of which the heavens will be dissolved, being on fire, and the elements will melt with fervent heat? ¹³ Nevertheless we, according to His promise, look for new heavens and a new earth in which righteousness dwells.

¹⁴ Therefore, beloved, looking forward to these things, be diligent to be found by Him in peace, without spot and blameless; ¹⁵ and consider that the longsuffering of our Lord is salvation—as also our beloved brother Paul, according to the wisdom given to him, has written to you, ¹⁶ as also in all his epistles, speaking in them of these things, in which are some things hard to understand, which untaught and unstable people twist to their own destruction, as they do also the rest of the Scriptures.

¹⁷ You therefore, beloved, since you know this beforehand, beware lest you also fall from your own steadfastness, being led away with the error of the wicked; ¹⁸ but grow in the grace and knowledge of our Lord and Savior Jesus Christ.

To Him be the glory both now and forever. Amen.

EXPLORATION

1. What does Peter state is his goal for writing his two letters to believers in Christ?

2. What is the value of recalling "the words spoken in the past by the holy prophets" (verse 2)?

_____

_____

_____

_____

3. Why is it important for believers to know what to expect in the last days?

_____

_____

_____

_____

4. For what reason does Peter say God is delaying his punishment of the wicked?

_____

_____

_____

_____

5. How can you be sure that God is really in control?

_____

_____

_____

6. In light of Jesus' imminent return, how should you lead your life?

_____

_____

_____

INSPIRATION

After the bombs of World War II ravaged downtown Warsaw, only one skeletal structure remained on the city's main street. The badly damaged structure was the Polish headquarters of the British and Foreign Bible Society, and the words on its only remaining wall were clearly legible from the street: "Heaven and earth will pass away, but my words will never pass away."

This is the picture of the Christian hope. Though the world may collapse, the work of Christ will endure. So, "see to it that you are not alarmed" (Matthew 24:6).

"See to it . . ." Bosses and teachers are known to use that phrase. "See to it that you fill out the reports." Or, "Your essay is due tomorrow. See to it that you finish your work." The words call for additional attention, special focus, extra resolve. Isn't this what Christ is asking of us? In this dangerous day, on this Fabergé-fragile globe, with financial collapse on the news and terrorists on the loose, we have every reason to retreat into bunkers of dread and woe.

But Christ says to us, "See to it that you are not alarmed." . . . "Be faithful, even to the point of death, and I will give you life as your victor's crown" (Revelation 2:10).

Make sure the hull of your convictions can withstand the stress of collisions.

Builders of the Titanic should have been so wise. The luxury liner sank because contractors settled for cheap rivets and suffered from poor planning. Rivets are the glue that hold the steel plates together. Facing a shortage of quality bolts, the builders used substandard ones that popped their heads upon impact with the iceberg.

How sturdy are the bolts of your belief? Reinforce them with daily Bible readings, regular worship, and earnest communion with God. "Courage is fear that has said its prayers."

And remember: "All these [challenging times] are the beginning of birth pains" (Matthew 24:8), and birth pangs aren't all bad. (Easy for me to say.) Birth pains signal the onset of the final push. The obstetrician assures the mom-to-be, "It's going to hurt for a time, but it's going to get better." Jesus assures us of the same. Global conflicts indicate our date on the maternity calendar. We are in the final hours, just a few pushes from delivery, a few brief ticks of eternity's clock from the great crowning of creation. A whole new world is coming! . . .

All things, big and small, flow out of the purpose of God and serve his good will. When the world appears out of control, it isn't. When warmongers appear to be in charge, they aren't. When ecological catastrophes dominate the day, don't let them dominate you. (From *Fearless* by Max Lucado.)

REACTION

7. How are you making sure the "hull of your convictions can withstand the stress of collisions"?

8. How sturdy are the "bolts of your beliefs"? How are you reinforcing your life with God's truth?

9. In what circumstances is it tempting to believe God is not in control?

10. Why do people often turn away from God when they need him the most?

_____

_____

_____

_____

11. How can you remind yourself of the truth that God is always in control the next time you feel disappointed or discouraged?

_____

_____

_____

12. What step of faith can you take to demonstrate your renewed trust in God?

_____

_____

_____

LIFE LESSONS

Peter told his readers he intended to "stir up their minds" with his two letters. He intends to "stir up our minds" as well. Every other aspect of our life in Christ depends on the reliability of God's Word and the assurance of Jesus' return. Waiting isn't easy. We may be tempted to accuse God of being slow in keeping his promise. But if we are learning to listen to his voice more and more clearly, we will hear what we need in his Word to keep us trusting. And we'll also find plenty to keep us busy while we're waiting for Christ's return!

DEVOTION

Father in heaven, thank you that you are patient with us and always in control. Teach us to surrender our fears and our burdens to you and leave them at your feet. And Father, we thank you that you always do what is best for us.

JOURNALING

In what areas of your life have you doubted that God had your best interests at heart?

_____

_____

_____

_____

_____

_____

_____

_____

_____

_____

_____

_____

FOR FURTHER READING

To complete the books of 1 and 2 Peter during this twelve-part study, read 2 Peter 3:1–18. For more Bible passages on trusting God, read 2 Chronicles 20:5–9; Psalm 20:7; Proverbs 3:5; Isaiah 12:2; Daniel 4:34–35; Nahum 1:7; Zephaniah 3:12; John 14:1–3; and Hebrews 2:13.

LEADER'S GUIDE FOR SMALL GROUPS

Thank you for your willingness to lead a group through *Life Lessons from 1 and 2 Peter*. The rewards of being a leader are different from those of participating, and we hope you find your own walk with Jesus deepened by this experience. During the twelve lessons in this study, you will guide your group through selected passages in 1 and 2 Peter and explore the key themes of the letters. There are several elements in this leader's guide that will help you as you structure your study and reflection time, so be sure to follow along and take advantage of each one.

BEFORE YOU BEGIN

Before your first meeting, make sure the group members have their own copy of the *Life Lessons from 1 and 2 Peter* study guide so they can follow along and have their answers written out ahead of time. Alternately, you can hand out the guides at your first meeting and give the group some time to look over the material and ask any preliminary questions. Be sure to send a sheet around the room during that first meeting and have the members write down their name, phone number, and email address so you can keep in touch with them during the week.

There are two ways to structure the duration of the study. You can choose to cover each lesson individually for a total of twelve weeks of discussion, or you can combine two lessons together per week for a total of six weeks of discussion. (Note that if the group members read the selected passages of Scripture for each lesson, they will cover the entire books of 1 and 2 Peter during the study.) The following table illustrates these options:

Twelve-Week Format

Week	Lessons Covered	Reading
1	A Living Hope	1 Peter 1:1–12
2	New Life in Christ	1 Peter 1:13–25
3	The Cornerstone	1 Peter 2:1–10
4	Following Jesus' Example	1 Peter 2:11–25
5	Holy Living	1 Peter 3:1–7
6	Loving People	1 Peter 3:8–22
7	Joyful Service	1 Peter 4:1–11
8	Trusting God Through Trials	1 Peter 4:12–19
9	Grace to the Humble	1 Peter 5:1–14
10	Self-Discipline	2 Peter 1:1–21
11	False Teachers	2 Peter 2:1–22
12	God Is in Control	2 Peter 3:1–18

Six-Week Format

Week	Lessons Covered	Reading
1	A Living Hope / New Life in Christ	1 Peter 1:1–25
2	The Cornerstone / Following Jesus' Example	1 Peter 2:1–25
3	Holy Living / Loving People	1 Peter 3:1–22
4	Joyful Service / Trusting God Through Trials	1 Peter 4:1–19
5	Grace to the Humble / Self-Discipline	1 Peter 5:1–14; 2 Peter 1:1–21
6	False Teachers / God Is in Control	2 Peter 2:1–3:18

Generally, the ideal size you will want for the group is between eight to ten people, which ensures everyone will have enough time to participate in discussions. If you have more people, you might want to break up the main group into smaller subgroups. Encourage those who show up at the first meeting to commit to attending the duration of the study, as this will help the group members get to know each other, create stability for the group, and help you know how to prepare each week.

Each of the lessons begins with a brief reflection that highlights the theme you will be discussing that week. As you begin your group time, have the group members briefly respond to the opening question to get them thinking about the topic at hand. Some people may want to tell a long story in response to one of these questions, but the goal is to keep the answers brief. Ideally, you want everyone in the group to get a chance to answer, so try to keep the responses to just a few minutes. If you have more talkative group members, say up front that everyone needs to limit his or her answer to two minutes.

Give the group members a chance to answer, but tell them to feel free to pass if they wish. With the rest of the study, it's generally not a good idea to have everyone answer every question—a free-flowing discussion is more desirable. But with the opening reflection question, you can go around the circle. Encourage shy people to share, but don't force them.

Before your first meeting, let the group members know how the lessons are broken down. During your group discussion time the members will be drawing on the answers they wrote to the Exploration and Reaction sections, so encourage them to always complete these ahead of time. Also, invite them to bring any questions and insights they uncovered while reading to your next meeting, especially if they had a breakthrough moment or if they didn't understand something they read.

WEEKLY PREPARATION

As the leader, there are a few things you should do to prepare for each meeting:

- *Read through the lesson.* This will help you to become familiar with the content and know how to structure the discussion times.
- *Decide which questions you want to discuss.* Depending on how you structure your group time, you may not be able to cover every

question. So select the questions ahead of time that you absolutely want the group to explore.

- *Be familiar with the questions you want to discuss.* When the group meets you'll be watching the clock, so you want to make sure you are familiar with the Bible study questions you have selected. You can then spend time in the passage again when the group meets. In this way, you'll ensure you have the passage more deeply in your mind than your group members.

- *Pray for your group.* Pray for your group members throughout the week and ask God to lead them as they study his Word.

- *Bring extra supplies to your meeting.* The members should bring their own pens for writing notes, but it's a good idea to have extras available for those who forget. You may also want to bring paper and additional Bibles.

Note that in many cases there will not be one "right" answer to the question. Answers will vary, especially when the group members are being asked to share their personal experiences.

STRUCTURING THE DISCUSSION TIME

You will need to determine with your group how long you want to meet each week so you can plan your time accordingly. Generally, most groups like to meet for either sixty minutes or ninety minutes, so you could use one of the following schedules:

Section	60 Minutes	90 Minutes
WELCOME (members arrive and get settled)	5 minutes	10 minutes
REFLECTION (discuss the opening question for the lesson)	10 minutes	15 minutes
DISCUSSION (discuss the Bible study questions in the Exploration and Reaction sections)	35 minutes	50 minutes
PRAYER/CLOSING (pray together as a group and dismiss)	10 minutes	15 minutes

As the group leader, it is up to you to keep track of the time and keep things moving along according to your schedule. You might want to set a timer for each segment so both you and the group members know when your time is up. (Note that there are some good phone apps for timers that play a gentle chime or other pleasant sound instead of a disruptive noise.) Don't feel pressured to cover every question you have selected if the group has a good discussion going. Again, it's not necessary to go around the circle and make everyone share.

Don't be concerned if the group members are silent or slow to share. People are often quiet when they are pulling together their ideas, and this might be a new experience for them. Just ask a question and let it hang in the air until someone shares. You can then say, "Thank you. What about others? What came to you when you reflected on the passage?"

GROUP DYNAMICS

Leading a group through *Life Lessons from 1 and 2 Peter* will prove to be highly rewarding both to you and your group members—but that doesn't mean you will not encounter any challenges along the way! Discussions can get off track. Group members may not be sensitive to the needs and ideas of others. Some might worry they will be expected to talk about matters that make them feel awkward. Others may express comments that result in disagreements. To help ease this strain on you and the group, consider the following ground rules:

- When someone raises a question or comment that is off the main topic, suggest you deal with it another time, or, if you feel led to go in that direction, let the group know you will be spending some time discussing it.
- If someone asks a question you don't know how to answer, admit it and move on. At your discretion, feel free to invite group members to comment on questions that call for personal experience.

- If you find one or two people are dominating the discussion time, direct a few questions to others in the group. Outside the main group time, ask the more dominating members to help you draw out the quieter ones. Work to make them a part of the solution instead of the problem.
- When a disagreement occurs, encourage the group members to process the matter in love. Encourage those on opposite sides to restate what they heard the other side say about the matter, and then invite each side to evaluate if that perception is accurate. Lead the group in examining other Scriptures related to the topic and look for common ground.

When any of these issues arise, encourage your group members to follow the words from the Bible: "Love one another" (John 13:34), "If it is possible, as far as it depends on you, live at peace with everyone" (Romans 12:18), and, "Be quick to listen, slow to speak and slow to become angry" (James 1:19).

Thank you again for taking the time to lead your group. May God reward your efforts and dedication and make your time together in this study fruitful for his kingdom.

ALSO AVAILABLE IN THE LIFE LESSONS SERIES

Now available wherever books and ebooks are sold.

Also Available in the Life Lessons Series